SCHOOL TREASURES

Architecture of Historic Boston Schools

DORIS COLE

and

NICK WHEELER

Photographer

Published by
Font & Center Press
P.O. Box 95
Weston, MA 02493
www.fontandcenter.com

Library of Congress Cataloging-in-Publication Data
Cole, Doris.
  School treasures : architecture of historic Boston schools /
Doris Cole and Nick Wheeler, photographer.
    p. cm.
  Includes bibliographical references and index.
  ISBN 1-883280-14-1
    1. School buildings—Massachusetts—Boston—
  Design and construction.   I. Title.

LB3218.M4 C65 2002
371.6'09744'61—dc21   2002017833

First Printing 2002
Printed in the United States of America
1   2   3   4   5   6   7   8   9   10

DEDICATION

Dr. Janice Ellen Cole, Ph.D.

July 25, 1936 — December 9, 1996

Teacher, Sister, Leader

PREVIOUS BOOKS BY DORIS COLE

From Tipi to Skyscraper:
A History of Women in Architecture
(1973)

Eleanor Raymond, Architect
(1981)

The Lady Architects:
Lois Lilley Howe, Eleanor Manning and Mary Almy, 1893–1937
(1990)
with Karen Cord Taylor

DONORS

Fleet Boston Financial Foundation

Anonymous Donor

Richard Mandelkorn

Wheeler Photographics

Cole and Goyette, Architects and Planners Inc.

ACKNOWLEDGMENTS

Thomas M. Menino, Mayor of Boston

Thomas W. Payzant, Superintendent, Boston Public Schools

Harold L. Goyette, AIA, AICP, Principal,
Cole and Goyette, Architects and Planners Inc.

Khadijah Abdus-Sabur, AIA,
Assistant Director of Facilities Management,
Boston Public Schools

Kenneth Caldwell, Chief of Staff, Boston Public Schools

John F. Cook, Photographer

Michelle Courton Brown,
President of Fleet Boston Financial Foundation

Frank Giuliani, Photographer

Anton Grassi, Photographer

Ilene Horowitz, Publisher, Font & Center Press, Inc.

Andrew Hudak, AIA, Deputy Director,
Boston Department of Neighborhood Development

Ira Jackson, Director of the Center for Business & Government,
JFK School of Government, Harvard University

Richard Mandelkorn, Photographer

Martha Pierce, Liaison to the Boston Public Schools, Mayor's Office

Antonia Pollak, Director of Environment, City of Boston

Andrew Puleo, Senior Engineer/Unit Leader, Boston Public Schools

Albert Rex, Executive Director, Boston Preservation Alliance

Steve Rosenthal, Photographer

Rob Roy, Director of Facilities Management, Boston Public Schools

Tobin Shulman, Co-author Assistant, Cole and Goyette

William T. Smith, Photographer

Dennis R. Valeri, Project Director/BPS Campbell Center

Peter Vanderwarker, Photographer

Charles Worcester, AIA, Assistant Director of Operations,
Boston Department of Neighborhood Development

PREFACE

Boston is blessed with wonderful architecture from the three-deckers of Dorchester to our American icons like Faneuil Hall. Sometimes overlooked, however, is the contribution of our public buildings such as libraries, municipal buildings, firehouses, courthouses, and schools.

This wonderful book of photographs and descriptions of Boston's schools illustrates the prominent place these well designed buildings hold in each neighborhood. I encourage each of you to take a second look at this unique part of Boston's heritage, its school buildings.

As Mayor, I continue to fulfill my pledge to restore the school system to a national symbol of excellence. We will continue to invest in these important buildings so that they may continue to serve the children of Boston.

Thomas M. Menino
Mayor of Boston

TABLE OF CONTENTS

CHAPTER 1
Exploring for Treasure

BOSTON IS ONE OF MANY CITIES AND TOWNS IN THE UNITED States (and throughout the world) that has historic buildings, including schools, to be admired, studied, preserved, and updated for future use. Across our country, in New York, Chicago, Mobile, San Francisco, and elsewhere, there are older buildings that are both beautiful and renewable resources for those communities. To explore the architectural treasures of the Boston public schools is to demonstrate in one city that which exists in many. These schools are valued by students, parents, teachers, administrators, educators, architects, preservationists, politicians, and neighbors. This book is for all of us as we appreciate the past and look towards the future.

The architectural treasures of the Boston public schools are the link to our past accomplishments and to our future potential. Both in plan and detail these buildings have been creatively designed and carefully crafted by architects and artisans. The superb plaster carvings in the auditorium of the Martin Luther King Jr. Middle School; the intricate stone tracery at the Brighton High School; the sumptuous wood carvings at the Jeremiah Burke High School; the fanciful limestone turrets at the East Boston High School; the colorful courtyard at the O'Hearn School, and the stunning auditorium at the Gardner School are only a few of the architectural gems at the Boston public schools.

The Boston public schools include about 129 buildings that were constructed in the late nineteenth century and throughout the twentieth century. They range from four schools of the 1890s; twenty-three schools of the 1920s; twenty-two schools of the 1930s; to twenty-four schools of the 1970s. Most of the schools have received additions, renovations, and rejuvenations to expand educational programs and to upgrade building systems. For example, the Gardner Elementary School originally constructed in 1906 received a classroom addition in 1958, a rejuvenation in 1993, and numerous renovations between those dates. Fortunately, throughout this process of renewal, many of the schools have been preserved and enhanced.

The first and oldest public school in America was founded in Boston, and we are proud of it. Boston Latin School began in 1635 to prepare young men for college. It continues as a coeducational school and is considered the jewel in the crown of the Boston public school system. Soon after the founding of the Boston Latin School, the first compulsory school law requiring a teacher for each community with fifty families was enacted in 1647. This emphasis upon public education for children continued and was the focus of Horace Mann's attention in 1837 as he established the state board of education in Massachusetts to strengthen educational standards in public schools.[1] Education has been of paramount importance in Boston leading to a mélange of public, private, parochial, and state chartered schools for primary and secondary education. The city and surrounding communities are filled with colleges, universities, law and medical schools, and music and art schools. Educational institutions such as Harvard, MIT, Boston University, Northeastern University, and the New England Conservatory of Music are part of the economic and cultural life of metropolitan Boston. In Boston, education defines the persona. Rarely is a speaker introduced without giving educational accomplishments, school ties, and a string of degrees. Our politicians proclaim their academic accomplishments, or head back to school to obtain degrees. For business leaders, as well as wayward youths, the local press includes academic affiliations. Our local economy is fueled by banking and finance as well as medical research and technological innovation. The American Dream that education is the path to success holds strong with each new wave of immigrants splashing upon the shores of Boston and this tradition of public schooling charts the future for their children.

You don't have to live in Boston to be a Bostonian. The city of Boston is the core of a metropolitan area with four million inhabitants. The adjacent cities and towns of Chelsea, Revere, Cambridge, Brookline, Newton, Dedham, and Milton are just a few of the communities that stretch out to Route 128 and beyond making up greater Boston. The Athens of the West and the Hub of the Universe are the descriptions of Boston by its ever modest inhabitants. What happens within the city economically, culturally, and educationally ripples out to affect the surrounding communities. Keeping the Hub spinning and the core solid is of major concern to greater Bostonians. Part of that health is the school system which is discussed and debated endlessly. The superintendent of the Boston public schools is sought as a speaker by business groups though many of those attending don't live in Boston or have children in the school system. The Boston School Committee, sometimes appointed and at other times elected, is a springboard for political careers in both city and state politics. The Boston business community is busy with partnerships, training programs, and grants to the various public schools. Some suburbanites who have fled Boston and cut their immigrant roots might scorn the city schools; the governor, the state legislators, and certainly the state board of education all have opinions, advice, and comments on the Boston schools. Yet with nearly 63,000 children—which is 75% of all school-age children in the city—attending public schools,[2] there is agreement that what happens in those school buildings will affect the future of all greater Bostonians.

Boston is called a city of neighborhoods, and the public schools are located within those neighborhoods stretching out far from the City Hall plaza covering old Scollay Square, the golden dome of the State Capital building on Beacon Hill, and the skyscrapers of the financial district on State Street. Few tourists venture out to the neighborhoods which are not on the Freedom Trail tour and are off the tourist map. Inhabitants of the adjacent towns come to central Boston to work and play, but rarely dive into the neighborhoods from the highways and thoroughfares that link their towns to central Boston. Many Bostonians know their own neighborhood, are familiar with a few other areas, and have heard tales and myths of the remaining. All of us begin our journeys through Boston with a map in our car to guide us through the maze of streets and squares, over hills and bridges, around ponds and parks. Though at times confused, we clearly remember that there is a Dorchester Street and a Dorchester Avenue, a Washington Street in Boston and a Washington Street in Dorchester, a South End and a South Boston and that those who forget the basic geographical facts of Boston might be lost for days. The map of Boston is strewn with little red dots marked E.S., M.S., H.S. denoting the elementary, middle, and high schools scattered across the city neighborhoods. It is the map of exploration, adventure, and discovery for the architectural treasures within the public schools of Boston.

Unlike most cities, Boston did not start with a small core and gradually build its streets, houses, and schools out to the present boundaries. Boston grew through the annexation of neighboring towns incorporating their communities with buildings, schools, parks, farms, cultures, local names, and identities. Founded in 1630 on a piece of land in Massachusetts Bay connected to the mainland by only the very narrow Roxbury Neck, the citizens of Boston soon began both filling and annexing land increasing the first 780 acres to over 28,019 acres. East Boston was annexed only seven years later in 1637 though its location across the Boston Inner Harbor continues to keep it physically separated from the rest of the city. The 1800s were busy years, starting with the annexation of South Boston in 1804; the filling of Back Bay begun in 1856; the annexation of Roxbury in 1868; the annexation of four communities—Charlestown, Dorchester, Brighton, and West Roxbury—in 1874; and finally the annexation of Hyde Park in 1912.[3] The pattern of these areas was even more intricate with names such as Orient Heights, Jamaica Plain, Allston, Roslindale, Mattapan, Lower Mills, and Readville further enriching the fabric of Boston. Most of the schools that came with these towns have since been demolished and replaced with other school buildings. However, the Rogers Middle School in Hyde Park, completed in 1902, predates the town's annexation by ten years. The Taft Middle School in Brighton and Clap Elementary School in Dorchester were built only about twenty years after those towns joined Boston. The various high schools, though more recent in construction, continue to proudly carry the names of their original towns: Brighton, Charlestown, Dorchester, East Boston, Hyde Park, South Boston, and West Roxbury.

As Boston increased its acreage, it also increased its general population and number of school-age children. This seaport on the Atlantic Ocean was and is a city of immigrants, beginning with Anglo-Saxon Puritans in the 1600s, Irish in the 1840s, Italians in the 1880s, Jews in the 1890s,[4] African-Americans in the 1950s, and continuing on with Chinese, Vietnamese, Russians, Haitians, Canadians, Armenians, Polish, and numerous other nationalities as the nations of the world collide and separate. In 1743, the population was 16,382 rising to 100,000 in the 1840s, 500,000 in the 1900s, and up to 801,444 in the 1950s. With a dip to 697,197 in 1960, it held steady with 589,141 in 2000. The increases in population soon filled the open areas between the annexed towns with people, houses, factories, shops, and schools. The people who came to Boston were more often poor than rich upon arrival, but they had the fare to get here, decided it was better than where they had left, joined in the fray of urban polyglot life, and shared in the shaping of Boston's evolving history. The neighborhoods were not all beautiful, spacious, or even tidy. There were slums, poverty, and filth. There were three-decker wood houses cheek-to-jowl that leaned precariously from the day they were built. Other blocks were filled with comfortable apartment buildings or had single-family houses, many small, some large, some with gardens. Often it was the school, red brick or stone, sturdy, dignified, built with care, decorated with carvings and murals, that stood firmly in these neighborhoods as life ebbed and flowed around them.

The construction of public schools in these ever evolving neighborhoods responded to the increases in population tempered by economics, politics, and wars. There was a surge of new schools constructed in the early 1900s to meet the needs of a growing population, but this was soon tempered by the demands of World War I. With prosperity in the 1920s and rising population, school construction started again and continued through the 1930s thanks to the New Deal's Public Works Administration. World War II brought new school construction to a total halt in the 1940s. Eventually in the late 1950s and 1960s a modest number of new schools were constructed while numerous older schools were demolished or closed as Boston's population declined nearly 15%.[5] With orders from the courts to equalize educational opportunities, more than two new schools per year were constructed in the 1970s, and existing school buildings were rejuvenated in the 1980s. As the 1990s raced towards the new century, plans for renovations, rejuvenations, additions, and new schools continued for a school system, a people, a city, and a history that is evolving, twisting, turning, changing through time.

The architectural designs for the public schools have responded to the various guidelines written by the City of Boston, the Commonwealth of Massachusetts, and the Federal government over a long period of time. In 1909, the Annual Report of the Schoolhouse Department described the plaster casts and framed pictures presented by the Boston School Art League to embellish the classrooms and enrich the learning experience. In 1916, the Schoolhouse Report included Standards for General Details with drawings for such items as storage cabinets, wardrobes, and bookcases. In 1928, the requirements for schools were further defined by the Boston Schoolhouse Department in Appendix VI, General Information as to Standard Requirements for

School Buildings and Yards. Sizes for classrooms; layouts for the print-ing, mechanical drawing, wood working, and pattern making shops; and details for benches, soapstone sinks, and exhibit board frames were scrutinized in this 1928 report. Codifying procedures continued in detail with the Standard Specifications for Interior Painting of 1950 selecting colors and requiring that plaster ceilings be given one coat of hot water calcimine. The continuously developing process moved on to the School Report of 1962 which guided the surge of new construction in the 1970s, and the Unified Facilities Plan for the 1980s, which upgraded and renovated existing schools through the Rebuilding Boston program. As the twentieth century proceeded towards the twenty- first, another Master Plan for Boston Schools was developed by the Department of Neighborhood Development and the Boston Public School Department. Each of these guidelines has reflected that partic-ular point in time in terms of preferred teaching methods, educational aspirations, general living standards, and societal needs.

The influence of the state board of education has increased tre-mendously since its beginnings in 1837 to collect and publicize school information throughout the state. With the end of World War II and the resulting postwar baby boom, cities and towns were hard pressed to meet the costs for new schools and turned to the state government for help. Chapter 645 of the Acts of 1948 eventually brought increased clout to the state board of education through its ability to provide monetary grants to local school departments. With these grants came standards and guidelines for the planning and construction of public elementary, middle, and high schools. Though general in scope, the size of classrooms and the types of other educational spaces were outlined and have profoundly affected the preservation of older schools and the design of new schools.

The federal government has also played its part in affecting the architectural designs for public schools in Boston, in Massachusetts, and throughout the nation. The Public Works Administration eventually paid 45% of the cost for construction of new schools in 1936, but, of course, with this money came suggestions, regulations, and reviews. In 1946, President Truman provided federal assistance to the school lunch programs, and suddenly, places were needed in the school buildings to cook and eat those meals. In 1974, Judge Garrity required regulations to achieve racially integrated schools, and areas for bus drop-offs and parking affected site acreage and design. Though many of the regulations over the years were not specifically architectural, they changed and modified the perceived adequacy of the schools.

We could engage in an endless discussion concerning pedagogical philosophies and teaching methods—and such discussions have continued for more than 360 years in Boston with each generation convinced that its views were the best. Perhaps those views were best for that particular generation of school children, but, if anything, history has demonstrated that future views will change and will even revert to former views. Children have sat in fixed seats bolted to the floor, in circles, squares, and groups. Teachers have been the focal point at the head of the class and as moving points around the room. They have taught as individuals and as teams for few children and many. Classrooms have been separate rooms with four walls and a door; have been clustered with movable walls; and have been open spaces with multiple levels and even conversation pits. Physical education has been accommodated in basement playrooms, gymnasia, outdoor play areas, and neighboring parks or not at all.

The daily drill at the chalkboard has been replaced by computers. The joy (or dread) of carrying the note to the principal's office has been replaced with the intercom. This book is not a discussion of reading levels, new math, phonetics, test scores, dress codes, busing, bilingual education, lunch menus, teachers unions, snow days, or the myriad of other items favored for heated debate in Boston. With a belief that educational methods have and will continue to change, this book explores the solutions devised for the problems and questions presented to the architects and artisans.

The architecture reflects, is influenced by, and is a part of its time in plan, design, materials, costs, placement, and esthetic taste. Originally constructed to meet one generation's aspirations, the buildings have been adapted to meet each new generation's dreams. With numerous renovations and additions, schools have grown, accommodated new curricula, and added amenities such as libraries and gymnasia. Available and momentarily fashionable materials have sometimes changed the red brick school house to the precast concrete and glass edifice; the granite trim to cast stone; and the wood roof trusses to steel. Interior finishes have changed from portland cement plaster to gypsum plaster, from various glazed tiles to painted concrete block and back again to gypsum plaster. Sites were generally small in the early 1900s for these urban schools and became larger in the 1970s. Even the New England climate persists in constantly changing from cold to hot and back again in one school day. Though all these variables might be confusing, they represent the factors that have brought both uniformity and variety to the designs for school buildings.

The architects and artisans have concentrated on transforming the mundane to the poetic. With a sense of proportion and scale, a bureaucratic list of room sizes has been transformed into handsome spaces for children, teachers, and community. Required egress doors have become stately portals welcoming students and visitors. Handrails have been crafted with special posts and spindles. Durable flooring has been translated into patterned multicolored polished terrazzo. Auditoria have been embellished with pilasters, friezes, and paneling. Medallions, pediments, and cornices invigorate the facades. Ornate wrought iron fences surround the sites. Murals enliven some walls. Even a fire escape becomes an opportunity for geometric playfulness in the hands of the artisan. A pride in one's work and a joy in creation have created architectural treasures that are a delight to our spirits.

The architectural styles selected for these school buildings reflect, in general, the architectural styles which were fashionable at that particular moment in time. However, the architectural vocabularies of these various styles developed pronounced Boston accents. In the nineteenth and early twentieth centuries, the classical style was deemed appropriate for bringing dignity and grandeur to our public buildings. Cornices, friezes, pediments, columns, and pilasters were part of this classical vocabulary. In Boston, this was soon translated into New England granite and limestone for the classical trim and red brick for the body, and everything else that might be conceivably built of red brick. The nineteenth century Bostonian's fondness for red brick houses and sidewalks flowed over the schools with red brick façades, play yards, fence posts, steps, and garden edging. The little red wood schoolhouse became the large red brick school building. The opulence of the 1920s introduced an eclectic array of architectural styles, though tempered by the Bostonian's conservative views of esthetics, decorum, and money. In the 1930s many architects abandoned the classical vocabulary creating a new architecture which incorporated the materials and motifs of expanded industry. At some of the Boston schools, such as the Burke High School, the design boldly embraces this brave new world. At many schools, the classical motifs and red brick continued, though modified by the economic hardships of the Great Depression. After World War II, and particularly in the 1970s, there was a decided break with traditional architecture throughout the United States, and even in Boston. Both in the architectural academies and in the architectural offices, contemporary design was embraced with its clean lines, limited decoration, asymmetrical plans, and new materials. The Boston public schools constructed after World War II and through the 1970s incorporated this vocabulary of contemporary architecture. In the 1980s, Boston avoided the postmodern style, since the emphasis was upon renovation and renewal of older schools. In the 1990s, two trends in architectural style were pursued by many architects: one trend continued contemporary design, while the other trend called for historical contextualism.

Architectural styles could be compared to languages. People write in English, French, Italian, Spanish, Chinese, and numerous other languages; it is the selection of the words and how those words are put together that make some books great. In this same way, an architectural style has a vocabulary similar to a language. It is what elements are selected and how those elements are put together that make delightful or mundane buildings. With this attitude in mind, we search out the architectural treasures which creatively use their selected architectural language whether it be classical, traditional, or contemporary. There are certainly situations where one architectural style is more appropriate than another due to climate, topography, function, and decade. Also, there continues to be a lingering question that the classical style based upon Western European civilization dating back to Greece might not be fully appropriate for our nation, the United States, and our polyglot citizens, with lineage outside of Western Europe, such as Jews, Russians, Chinese, Africans, and Indians. In a sense, contemporary architecture tries to answer that question by creating a style that has the potential of being more reflective of America. Hopefully, our Boston accents continue to be strong enough to mold all architectural styles to suit our varied voices.

History is part of Boston, and our architecture is part of that history. Paul Revere's ride, the Boston Tea Party, the battle of Bunker Hill, and many other events are part of our legends, myths, and realities. When we look at central Boston and its neighborhoods, there are reminders of those early events in the names of streets, landmarks, and some buildings. Scattered through central Boston and the neighborhoods are eighteenth-century buildings such as Bulfinch's State Capital building on Beacon Hill, Christ Church in the North End, and the Shirley-Eustis House in Roxbury. There are acres of land covered with nineteenth-century buildings in the Back Bay, the South End, South Boston, Brighton, Charlestown, and the other neighborhoods. These sturdy brick buildings include townhouses, offices, shops, and civic institutions. But Boston is not static; it has a history and a future. The life of the city moves on and with this buildings are torn down and rebuilt. The public school buildings reflect our evolving history perhaps more strongly than any other group of buildings in Boston. Though nineteenth-century Boston thrives, only four public schools have survived in nineteenth-century buildings. From 1924 to 1964, seventy-nine older school buildings were demolished and another sixty-eight were sold for other uses.[6] Much has been lost, some good and some bad, in the demise of these public schools. It is possible that there were some unacknowledged architectural beauties that were lost, demolished, discarded, sold, removed, or abandoned. However, this book looks to our current and future history and, therefore, has sought out the living treasures in active public schools.

It is the health of these living treasures that is of concern. Some are barely breathing, but fortunately, many are alive and well. There have been cycles of injury and recovery. For example, the exteriors of the schools have been subjected to graffiti; then the graffiti has been covered with paint; and eventually both the graffiti and the paint have been removed to reveal again the sturdy beauty of the original brick and stone. Some architectural elements have faired less well due to the costs and difficulties of maintenance. For example, skylights have been roofed over, transforming light and airy spaces into rather gloomy rooms, while we all wait for the future development of the economical leakproof skylight. Often, what might appear to be neglect has actually preserved friezes, moldings, paneling, murals, and much more. Sometimes it is the quest for improvement and progress that can be detrimental to these buildings such as systems for computers, video, security, more lights and outlets, fire alarms, smoke detectors, and intercoms that sprout reams of conduit up walls and across ceilings of corridors and classrooms. With this book, it is our goal to encourage restorative care for the buildings that are less well by illustrating those that enjoy relatively good health.

Not every building is an architectural masterpiece though it might be filled with fine memories and function well as an academic institution. Consequently, this book is not a compendium of every public school building in Boston. We have had the delightful experience of exploring and searching, of finding both the obvious and the hidden. As with most explorers, we have had our guides. People in Boston have opinions on architecture and the school teachers, principals, students, parents, custodians, and administrators are not exceptions. They know what they have and know what they like. We have been led away proudly to see murals, light fixtures, terrazzo floors, stone and wood carvings, wardrobes, and boot warmers. These proud and hospitable people have allowed us to wander into nooks and crannies in search of the hidden. Since the majority of these schools were constructed in the early 1900s or before World War II, it was long before many of the current Bostonians were born or came to the city. However, these architectural treasures have become part of the cultural heritage, which they preserve, enjoy, and admire while planning for the future.

Please join us in our exploration. This book illustrates the riches we have found in Boston public schools and, undoubtedly, we have missed some, perhaps your favorites. Let us know or keep your treasures hidden if you wish. Our search has made us realize that there are distinguished schools in many towns and cities in Massachusetts and throughout the United States. Hopefully, you will enjoy your quest in your own home town as much as we have enjoyed our search in Boston. Now, with map in hand, we begin the adventure of discovery filled with surprise, delight, and mystery. Welcome to the expedition.

FOOTNOTES

1. Kelley, Walt, *What They Never Told You About Boston* (Camden, Maine, Down East Books, 1993) pp. 16, 21, 22, 25.

2. Boston Public Schools, *The Boston Public Schools at a Glance*, BPS Facts, No 1, March 1999.

3. *Encyclopaedia Britannica*, (Chicago, Encyclopaedia Britannica, Inc., William Benton, Publishers, 1962) Volume 3, pp. 933–938.

4. Trout, Charles H., Boston, *The Great Depression and the New Deal* (New York, Oxford University Press, 1977).

5. Wallace, Floyd, Associates, Inc., B*oston Public Facilities Overview,* January 14, 1994, Phase 1: Volume 2, Inventory and Conditions Report, p. 3.

6. *Annual Report*, December 31, 1964, Department of School Buildings, City Document No. 20, Appendix II, p. 40.

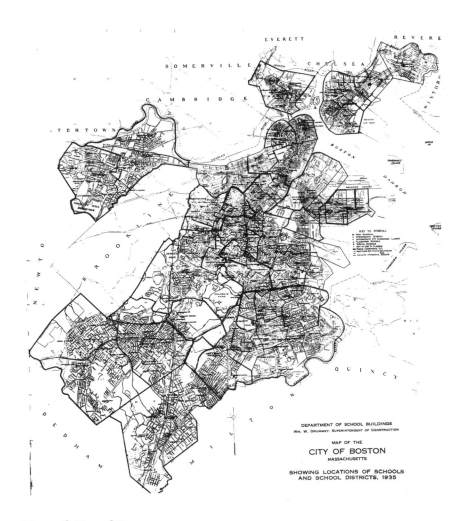

Map of City of Boston
Annual Report of the Department of School Buildings
January 1, 1935 to December 31, 1935

This oddly shaped city was divided by the Charles River and Boston Harbor with two neighborhoods, Charlestown and East Boston, to the north of these water barriers. Independent Brookline, that decided not to join the city's government, protruded into the urban mass almost separating Brighton from the rest of Boston.

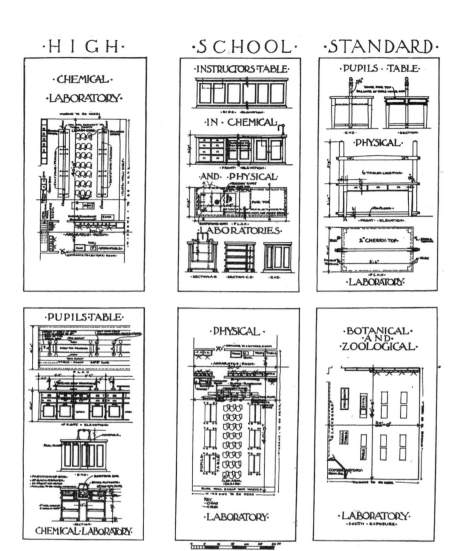

High School Standard Fittings
Annual Report of the Schoolhouse Department
February 1, 1905 to February 1, 1906

It was remarkable and noteworthy that Boston was planning and building such advanced high schools at the turn of the century. Boston was leading the nation in providing public high schools with well-equipped science laboratories. For example, the chemical laboratory was equipped with numerous fume hoods; laboratory benches with gas, water, and drainage troughs; and other conveniences.

Illustration courtesy of Boston Public Schools.

CHAPTER II

Turning the Century

T HE TURNING OF A CENTURY IS AN EXCITING TIME—SPARKING people's imaginations to envision the future and take stock of the past. President William McKinley expressed the optimistic politician's view to Congress on December 3, 1900.

> At the outgoing of the old and the incoming of the new century you begin the last session of the Fifty-Sixth Congress with evidence on every hand of individual and national prosperity and proof of the growing strength and increasing power for good of Republican institutions.[1]

Contrary to President McKinley's glowing assessment, the years before 1900 were tumultuous for our nation and people. It was only thirty-five years since the Civil War had ended. Though the Union was still whole and the slaves were finally free, the wounds were not healed and the African-Americans had not achieved equality. The economy had not been stable for twenty-five years with two depressions (1873 to 1877 and 1893 to 1897), with conflicts between labor and capitalists, bank closings, and long bread lines.[2] In addition to this economic instability, there was significant economic inequality in the last half of the nineteenth century. A study in 1890 reported that seven-eighths of American families held only one-eight of the wealth and that one percent of the people owned more than ninety-nine percent of the wealth. Though statistics varied slightly from Milwaukee to Boston over the decade, in 1900 about eighty percent of our people were living a marginal existence while the other twenty percent owned the assets of our nation.[3] Attention to economic and social woes had been diverted momentarily by the successes of the Spanish-American war, but the turning of the century refocused our nation's conscience towards building a new, more acceptable reality.

The Boston intellectuals also assessed the closing of the nineteenth century with optimistic admiration. Mary Caroline Crawford, author of numerous books by the turn of the century, wrote that the "high notes struck in the nineteenth century" could be "notes upon which we of the twentieth century may well workout a life-symphony."[4] Her observations of Boston culture in her 1910 book, *Romantic Days of Old Boston*, included admiration for the literary feminist Margaret Fuller; the abolitionist William Lloyd Garrison; the agitator Wendell Phillips; the preacher Theodore Parker; the Superintendent of Women Nurses Dorthea Dix; the colonel of the colored Fifty-Fifth Massachusetts Infantry Robert Gould Shaw; and the liberal causes that these Bostonians represented. She gamely wrote:

> *Steel said of a certain lady that to have known and loved her was a liberal education; to have shared in Boston's life and loved what it stood for during the nineteenth century was a liberal education.*[5]

Though Mary Crawford's rose-colored spectacles remained firmly in place as she reinforced the traditional tales of tea-sipping Bostonian liberal intellectuals, she was not blind to the realities which these proper Bostonians discussed or ignored so eloquently. She admonished Mayor Josiah Quincy for closing the very successful High School for Girls established in 1825, accusing him of bigotry towards females in general and Irish girls in particular; she cried out that "for the first time, we catch a glimpse of that anti-Irish-Catholic feeling which culminated in the burning of the Ursuline Convent in 1834."[6] She and other Bostonians knew that their liberal education from the nineteenth century encompassed both bad and good examples for the coming twentieth century.

This was a period of population growth in Boston with an increase to 500,000 people in the 1900s. Most of the annexation of neighboring communities had been completed by 1874 with the inclusion of Charlestown, Dorchester, Brighton, and West Roxbury in that year. Hyde Park was to join Boston soon after the turn of the century in 1912.[7] The increases in population were augmented by the birthrate creating large families and the major waves of immigrants from European countries. The potato famines in Ireland brought ten thousand Irish to Boston between 1830 and 1835 and more in the 1840s. As the nineteenth century progressed and conditions in Europe regressed, Italians, Jews, and Eastern and Southern Europeans came to America and Boston to escape poverty, pogroms, and punishments. By 1900, Boston was no longer Anglo-Saxon; fifty percent of the population was of foreign stock; the majority of the population was foreign born or children of immigrants; many of the immigrants did not speak any English; and food, customs, clothing, and cultures became an exotic mixture to old

Boston's eyes and ears. This growing population spread out through the annexed communities to the expanded borders of Boston carried by the increasingly popular streetcars to Dorchester, Roxbury, West Roxbury, and Brighton.[8]

The vision of the twentieth century for Boston and the nation was based upon both ideals and realities. There was that uniquely American optimism shared by the old and new immigrants that life would and could get better; and since no one was willing to give up his share of the pie, it meant that life must get better for all people, rich or poor. As Harold Faulkner explained, "to many thoughtful men in the opening years of the twentieth century it seemed that America in making her fortune was in peril of losing her soul."[9] There seemed to be three major issues which included social and work conditions, women's rights, and the well-being of children. These issues were based upon the realities of the day and, of course, would be refined and changed as the twentieth century progressed. Certainly there was not agreement about the issues or the solutions. Though perhaps most people found social and work conditions of the poor majority to be unacceptable, the solutions ranged from intermittent charity, new household inventions, and mechanized factories, to labor unions, socialism, and higher wages; revolution, anarchy, and communism were to be avoided. The issue of women's rights had been brought forward at Seneca Falls in 1848, strengthened by Bostonian Lucy Stone in 1850, and carried on forcefully by Susan B. Anthony until her death in 1906 when other suffrage leaders took up the struggle to gain the right to vote for women; amazingly it took well into the twentieth century before this issue was resolved affirmatively.

The third issue, the well-being of children, was the most representative of our nation's vision. America looked to the future and the future was its children. It was through the children that the vast variegated immigrant mass could be woven into a unified whole. Since many immigrants might not reach their own goals, opportunities for their children became even more important. Since earlier settlers often distrusted the ways of new immigrants, the training of those children became a societal care. For different reasons, there seemed to be common agreement upon the welfare of children encompassing their physical health, mental education, and moral fortitude. Of course, there were various opinions about means and methods to achieve this goal. Boston was in the forefront in 1894 as the first to establish a regular system of medical inspection for school children. By 1898, Massachusetts and many of the older industrial states had child-labor laws, but these were strengthened with the 1904 National Child Labor Committee and subsequent legislation limiting hours, increasing age, and trying to insure a basic level of literacy. In 1869, Massachusetts was among the earliest to address the needs of children by providing separate trials within the court system. In 1908, Massachusetts encouraged cities and towns to establish playgrounds for children that would provide active physical recreation and hopefully distraction from delinquent criminal activities.[10] However, it was education within the public schools that was considered to be most important towards the well-being of children for the twentieth century.

Education in the United States was revolutionary. It was unlike all concepts left behind in Europe. The United States was the first country to provide elementary and secondary schools that were truly free. It was extraordinary to assume, allow, and even demand that poor children attend school and learn the same lessons as other children. It was breathtaking to imagine that these young people might graduate to jobs that were beyond their parents' economic and social level. This was not the situation in most of Europe in the nineteenth century. For example, in England it was 1890 before tuition fees were not charged in most of their elementary schools; this meant the poor families unable to afford the tuition or to give up the child's income producing labor often did not send their children to school; this meant that these young people and their descendants would remain in jobs at or beneath their parents' level.[11] In America, all of this changed dramatically for the earlier settlers and particularly for the immigrants' children at the turn of the century.

Boston and Massachusetts were the leaders in this American educational revolution. As early as 1642, the General Court of Massachusetts made it the duty of parents and masters to teach children in their care both a trade and basic reading. In 1635, Boston had already established the Boston Latin School and then in 1639 took the remarkable step of establishing the first free public elementary school in America named after Richard Mather. In the 1830s, the first Boston public school for African-American children was opened on Beacon Hill at 46 Joy Street; and in 1844, Boston's first integrated public school for white and black boys was begun at the Phillips Grammar School on Pinckney Street.[12] In 1852, Massachusetts passed the first compulsory attendance law requiring all children to go to school. In addition to these earlier laws, the city was very busy constructing buildings so that the growing population of Boston would really have schools for their children. The Schoolhouse Department, also, was developing design standards for heating and plumbing systems, classroom sizes and plans, and bookcases and wardrobe fittings that were to be used at each school. At the beginning of the century, Boston was continuing its goal to provide similar public educational opportunities for all of its children.

Public education became more than teaching the three Rs—reading, writing, and arithmetic–in Boston and America. Educators and concerned citizens looked to the schools to alleviate and mitigate the detrimental influences of industrialization and urbanization; inundation by millions of immigrants; declining influence of the church upon the home; relaxation of parental discipline; and the living conditions of crowded slums.[13] Schools were to instill in children the moral guidelines for overcoming life's hardships as well as the mental training for productive occupations. How this was to be accomplished was, of course, discussed with various solutions advocated by educators. By the 1890s, city schools, including Boston, had developed an eight-year system for elementary schools with an organization of superintendent, principals, and teachers; graded levels of instruction; similar courses in all schools of the system; and an emphasis on order, efficiency, attendance, and punctuality.[14] This was also a period of expansion with the common school plan encompassing both elementary and secondary schools, which would be free and open to all children. By 1900, the majority of Boston children completed primary school, and attendance at high schools was increasing dramatically.

The schoolhouse design standards developed in Boston reflected the educational system and philosophy at the turn of the century. For example, the reading-writing-arithmetic curriculum had been expanded to include history, geography, physiology, nature study, drawing, manual training, home economics, and various other subjects. The plans for

Boston grammar schools included sewing rooms, cooking rooms, and manual training for children in grades one through eight. Physical exercise was strongly recommended for healthy children by noted educators, and this was reflected in the Boston school plans with separate exercise rooms for boys and girls on the ground floors. By the 1890s, kindergartens were advocated for young children, but in Boston this was to gain support at a later date. For older children, high schools were becoming more popular among city youths aspiring to white collar jobs within this thriving metropolis. In 1821, Boston established the new type of high school, English Classical School, which included both classical and modern academic subjects. By 1906, the Boston Schoolhouse Department had issued high school standards for chemistry, physical, botanical, and zoological laboratories, as well as an art drawing room with even a round model stand. As educational philosophy changed, the existing Boston schools were modified and new ones added to meet these changing educational needs.

In the late 1800s, American and Boston architects were designing public buildings in a variety of architectural styles. Most architects were looking back, not forward, reviving styles of former times. There was Renaissance Revival, Romanesque Revival, Classical, Gothic, and Queen Anne selected to express the building's function, the architect's esthetic and, at times, the client's whim. Boston shared in this revival frenzy on a huge scale with the 1860s design of Back Bay on a French model with grand boulevards, such as Commonwealth Avenue, over the recently filled land. Romanesque Revival was skillfully employed at Trinity Church in 1872 by architect H.H. Richardson and greatly admired by Bostonians. Facing the Romanesque Trinity Church across Copley Square rose the new Boston Public Library in 1895 in a totally different style, Renaissance Revival, ably designed by McKim Mead and White.[15] A few blocks away, Ralph Waldo Emerson's nephew, architect William Ralph Emerson, created the 1882 Boston Art Club building in Queen Anne Revival, which much later in the 1970s became a Boston public school, the Snowden International High School.

In 1893, the Columbian Exposition in Chicago set the stage for architecture from the East Coast to the West Coast. The stage set was Classical Revival for this idealized urban environment. It was composed of broad esplanades, ponds, and fountains artfully placed along the Lake Michigan shore by landscape architect, Fredrick Law Olmstead of Boston. It was filled with permanent and temporary buildings with exhibitions on contemporary and future worlds. The Women's Building was designed by Sophia Hayden, who had received her architectural degree from the Massachusetts Institute of Technology in 1890. Francis Bellamy, editor of *Youth's Companion*, wrote the Pledge of Allegiance to the flag that was recited by school children nationwide on the opening day of the exposition, Columbus Day, October 12, 1892, and has continued for more than a hundred years. Classical Revival architecture was embraced by professionals nationwide for public buildings. In Boston, the 1900 Symphony Hall by McKim Mead and White and Horticultural Hall by Wheelwright and Haven used the classical vocabulary; in 1909, the new Museum of Fine Arts by Gay Lowell did the same. Though not explicitly required by the Boston Schoolhouse Department, Boston public schools were styled in the Classical Revival tradition for the next decade.

The architects of Boston public schools were distinguished members of their profession in the early 1900s. They designed mansions, bridges, colleges, courthouses, post offices, churches, office towers, theaters, and clubs that are considered important to the city's architectural heritage. For example, E.M. Wheelwright, who designed the 1892 Fuller School and 1895 Taft School, was also the architect for the 1907 Longfellow Bridge, 1901 Horticultural Hall, 1901 New England Conservatory of Music and Jordan Hall. He even crossed the river to Cambridge to work his whimsical magic on the Lampoon Building at Harvard College in 1909. The 1904 Perry School architects, Clough & Wardner, used the French empire revival style when designing the Suffolk County Court House in 1896. After designing the Mather School in 1905, the architectural firm of Cram, Goodhue & Ferguson gained national fame for their gothic revival colleges, as well as their modern art deco 1947 John Hancock Tower with the flashing weather beacon. Architect E.T.P. Graham successfully made the transition from the small 1909 Everett Elementary School to the large 1914 City Hall Annex on Court Street in downtown Boston. Three landmark buildings in the Back Bay—the 1912 Harvard Club on Commonwealth Avenue, the 1904 Tennis & Racquet Club, and the 1905 Fenway Artist's Studios—were designed by Parker, Thomas & Rice, architects for the 1909 Hale Elementary School. Most of these architects made the transition graciously between the elaborate larger scale urban buildings and the smaller, more restrained neighborhood schools.

Though the classical revival style selected for the Boston public schools looked to the past, the materials and systems were decidedly contemporary. Sturdy, durable materials were selected that would be long lasting with hard use by hundreds of school children. Old wood schools were abandoned or demolished. Exteriors became red brick with stone or brick trim. Windows were large, multipaned wood-frame double-hung windows providing light and air to every classroom. The buildings had electrical light fixtures hung from the ceilings to supplement the natural daylight. Central heating for the cold New England winters was provided by large coal burning furnaces in the basements and cast iron steam radiators in each classroom. These state of the art engineering systems included gravity air ventilation ducts running up vertically through the building to the roof. Large toilet rooms for the students had slate toilet partitions, hot and cold running water, and marble lavatory bowls with brass brackets and traps. The building structures were brick bearing walls with concrete, and steel floor structures. Interior partitions were hollow clay tiles covered with Portland cement plaster.[16] Everything was up to date in Boston, and the city was building to last another century.

Boston progressed from planning for the new century to realizing those goals in the first decade of the twentieth century. The new Schoolhouse Department formed in 1901 quickly went to work to formulate citywide school standards, to implement those standards, and to construct new schools in the Boston neighborhoods of Brighton, South Boston, Dorchester, Roxbury, and East Boston. They reached out to meet the needs of the growing population of children within the city and to fulfill the requirements of an industrialized society for a literate workforce. There was a respect for history in the sense that they tried to build for future history. In fact, they were remarkably successful. One hundred years have passed, and twenty schools constructed around the turn of the last century were still serving as public schools at the turn of the next century. Four of these schools were built before 1900. The Rogers Middle School from 1902 was transferred to Boston in 1912 along with the town of Hyde Park. Most of the others were planned and constructed by the Schoolhouse Department and their prestigious private architects. Boston faced reality, developed solutions, and was moving forward to the seemingly bright potential of the early twentieth century.

FOOTNOTES

1. Time-Life Books Editors, *This Fabulous Century* 1900–1910, *Volume* I (New York, Time Life Books, 1971) p. 6.

2. Faulkner, Harold Underwood, A *History of American Life*: *Volume* XI, A *Quest for Social Justice*: 1898–1914 (New York, The MacMillan Company, 1931) p. 1.

3. Ibid, p. 21.

4. Crawford, Mary Caroline, *Romantic Days in Old Boston* (Boston, Little, Brown and Company, 1910) p. vii.

5. Ibid, p. vi.

6. Ibid, p. 9.

7. *Encyclopaedia Britannica*, (Chicago, Encyclopaedia Britannica, Inc., William Benton, Publishers, 1962) volume 3, pp. 933–938.

8. Whitehill, Walter Muir, *Boston*: A *Topographical History* (Cambridge, The Belknap Press of Harvard University, 1968) p. xx.

9. Faulkner, Opus ibid, pp. xv, xvi.

10. Faulkner, Opus ibid, pp. 180–188.

11. Encyclopaedia, Opus ibid, volume 8, p. 344.

12. Southworth, Susan and Michael, *The Boston Society of Architects'* AIA *Guide to Boston* (Chester, Connecticut, The Globe Pequot Press, 1992) p. 188.

13. Faulkner, Opus ibid, p. 188

14. Schlereth, Thomas J., *Victorian America*: *Transformations in Everyday Life*, 1876–1915 (New York, Harper Collins Publishers, 1991) p. 245.

15. Southworth, Opus ibid.

16. *Annual Reports of the Schoolhouse Department*, from 1901 through 1925.

· STANDARDS · OF · GENERAL · DETAIL ·
~ CITY · OF · BOSTON ~ SCHOOLHOUSE ~ DEPARTMENT ~

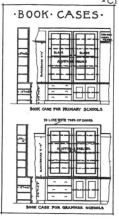

·BOOK · CASES·

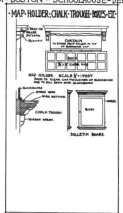

·MAP · HOLDER · CHALK · TROUGH · BOXES · ETC·

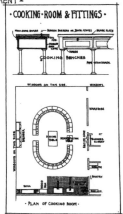

·COOKING · ROOM & FITTINGS·

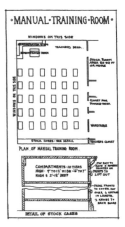

·MANUAL · TRAINING · ROOM·

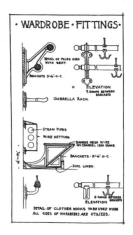

· WARDROBE · FITTINGS·

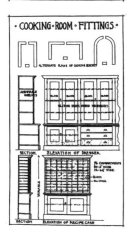

·COOKING · ROOM · FITTINGS·

Standards of General Detail
Annual Report of the Schoolhouse Department
January 31, 1903 to February 1, 1904

Established by the Acts of 1901, Chapter 473, the new Schoolhouse Department moved quickly to establish standards for primary and grammar schools. The standards reflected the current educational philosophy which provided manual training for boys and cooking for girls in grammar schools. As shown on the drawing titled "Book Cases," the height for the blackboards was lower for the primary schools than for the grammar schools. The "Wardrobe Fittings" were meticulously detailed with a floor rack and steam pipes to dry wet winter boots. This same attention to detail was found in the "Chalk Trough" with the hinged wire netting to keep the eraser out of the chalk dust. *Illustration courtesy of Boston Public Schools*

CHAPTER III

Growing Up

T HE DECADE BETWEEN 1910 AND 1920 WAS A PERIOD OF GROW-
ing up into maturity for our nation in general and Boston in
particular. The sobering events of war and plague affected us socially,
intellectually, and economically. World War I and the influenza epidemic
were to transform our relationship with foreign nations and our concept of ourselves. These attitudinal changes would in turn affect educational curricula and public school buildings. The period between
1910 and 1920 was complex, subtle, sometimes twisted, and other
times confused; it was our national adolescence as we explored who we
were and defined our place in the world order. At the turn of the century, Boston had gathered together its enormous immigrant population
and had striven to form a cohesive literate citizenry through its public
schools. With youthful energy, this was done quite successfully; the former immigrants had become established citizens. But pressures and
demands were changing; the question was now how these new citizens
would define their goals and deal with world events. The years surrounding World War I, the events and decisions, the actions and
reactions, and the effects and consequences would mold our national
character and our educational system.

Americans were spiritually and essentially neutral as World War I
began to roar through Europe. This war between Germany and the
Entente nations (France, England, Belgium, Russia, Italy, and others)
began in August 1914 and continued until November 1918; the United
States did not enter the war until 1917. From the outbreak of war to the
sinking of the British passenger ship, Lusitania, in 1915, Americans
were not very interested in becoming involved in a European conflict.[1]
The recent immigrants had purposefully left that continent behind to
join and shape a new nation. There were historic animosities and
resentments: the English-Americans and Irish-Americans disliked
England and its imperial ways; German-Americans and many Jews
resented Russia and its oppressive mandates; and most everyone could
remember injustices and inequalities. The sinking of the Lusitania and
other aggressive actions by Germany towards American foreign commerce enraged our free spirited citizens and any lingering sympathies
for Germany soon ended.[2] By 1916, our country was preparing for the
possibility of war; Congress had adopted a three-year building program
for the Navy and increases to the Army and National Guard.[3] Finally in

1917, the United States entered World War I—the war to end all wars.

The United States, and Boston along with it, profited from the war in Europe. Though there was much unemployment during the winter of 1914 and some gloomy financial forecasts, the economy perked up as war orders arrived from the Entente nations.

> By 1916, *the neutral United States had become the principal foreign munitions depot for Entente. The iron and steel exports of the United States more than doubled from 1914 to 1916 and almost doubled again in 1918.*[4]

The lack of German competition helped some industries, such as dyes, optical glass, drugs, and chemicals. As the war preparedness progressed, ship building increased. Women went to work in the factories making gas masks and airplanes and operating the wireless telegraphy. By the time the United States entered the war on April 6, 1917, skilled workers had been trained in the schools and were in place at the factories; physics, mathematics, science, and chemistry were producing product innovators. But the prewar prosperity was tempered by rising prices, inflation, and frequent strikes by trade unions for higher wages. Both the prosperity and unrest were to continue after the war.

The shocking experiences of World War I were intensified by the influenza epidemic of 1918. At the front, soldiers experienced gassed lungs; rats in the trenches; mutilated bodies; blown up villages; and the stench of death. Added to this was the flu that attacked both soldiers and civilians killing more than twenty-two million people. Sweeping across Asia, Europe, and then America, it killed many more than the bullets of the war. Boston was not immune to the ravages of the influenza epidemic and by early October all Boston schools were closed. Francis Russell in his 1964 book, *The Great Interlude*, still clearly remembered his curious terror as an eight-year-old third grader at the Martha Baker School in Mattapan as the death rate rose in Boston and the hearses to the cemeteries near his school increased during September 1918.

> In the line-storm days as we sat at attention with folded hands while Miss Sykes read the Bible lesson under the fly-spotted flag . . . we could

hear the carriages passing outside, the clop of horses' hooves in the wet leaves, or the swish of vacuum-cap tires above the rain trickling in the gutters.[5]

This influenza epidemic reminded people that the world was tied together by unselected events beyond war, trade, and migrations. How to protect one's country and children would become a question for this maturing society.

Changing war-time immigration and economic patterns affected society's goals for education. In 1913, there were 100,000 immigrants arriving in Massachusetts and 21,000 of these were Jews escaping from Poland.[6] By 1915, immigration was greatly reduced due to the European war. In 1917, literacy requirements were introduced for immigrants, and in 1921, immigration was limited by law.[7] Due to this marked decrease in immigration, the goals of education changed; it was no longer necessary to concentrate upon acclimating foreign children to American ways. The reduced population growth and the increased war economy brought new opportunities for women in business and skilled workers in factories. The educational curriculum was modified to reflect the needs of a war-time economy. The study of the German language was removed, and military training was introduced in many high schools. By 1918, all states had enacted compulsory education statutes at the high school level.[8] The Boston Schoolhouse Department had led the way in 1906 by issuing high school building standards and updating these standards in 1911. The needs of the industrialized New England economy were addressed with chemical, physical, zoological, and botanical laboratories as well as technical and commercial classrooms. With the end of World War I, the patterns of restricted immigration, increased economic opportunities, and the need for a high school education continued.

Both prosperity and inflation influenced the development of American schools. The strong prewar economy, the short duration of our involvement in World War I, and the economic strength after the war allowed school construction to continue almost without interruption. During 1917–1918, there was control of wartime goods and large public school building projects were suspended in New York City.[9] But in Boston, construction seemed to proceed on, though at a reduced rate, producing eleven schools that continued in use in the 1990s and many others that have been abandoned. Nationally, real income increased 28.7% between 1914 and 1926; and the enormously wealthy eased their conscience by contributing $37,095,290 to education in 1916 and increasing this to $126,873,032 in 1926.[10] However, with this prosperity came inflation, which was difficult on school budgets and teachers with slowly rising salaries. By the early twentieth century, many men had left teaching for higher-paid positions in business and women (who had fewer opportunities) filled classrooms as dedicated teachers. With prosperity, aspirations increased for both the middle class and the poor who aspired to join the middle class through education.

The United States continued to develop its revolutionary concept of education before, during, and after World War I. Our common education with opportunities for all children to go through elementary school and proceed to high school was unknown in Europe. For our nation, the demands of World War I strengthened the educational concept by increasing the demand for a high school education. For Europe, the social changes wrought by World War I strained their societies and educational dual plan systems. For example, in England there were no publicly maintained secondary schools until after 1902. By 1914, there were secondary schools but these were entered by competitive exams, often tuition was charged, and they were primarily preparation for university or high-level white-collar jobs.[11] In Europe, a person's future was decided when he was a child in elementary school. The decision to send him to secondary school or to trade school sealed his fate for life. In Europe, the educational system closed doors. In the United States, the educational system was expanding to provide young people with varied paths towards economic, social, and intellectual fulfillment.

The objectives for public education continued to be broad reaching on both the national and local level. The United States Commission on the Reorganization of Secondary Education 1918 Report recommended seven objectives: health, command of fundamental processes, worthy home membership, vocation, civic education, worthy use of leisure, and ethical character.[12] Boston not only embraced but also led the way in these national goals. Before the turn of the century, the city had introduced medical inspections for school children; in 1908, there were experimental gardens planted and tended by the urban school children; in 1909, the Open Air School on the roof of the Franklin Park Refectory Building served sickly children. The Boston School Art League attended to the children's culture by donating plaster casts and pictures for the classrooms. Many of these remain in the schools and more have been added through class gifts. The art work generally depicted classical scenes often with Greek gods and goddesses, horses, and chariots. In 1915, health issues were addressed again by the Boston Schoolhouse Department through their Plumbing Standards designed and illustrated with very specific details for running traps, tide traps, catch basins, slate and soapstone sinks, slate urinals, lavatory bowls, and water closets.[13] The American urge for moral guidance was described with sympathetic humor by Preston William Slosson in his book, The Great Crusade and After 1914–1918.

> There was constant pressure on school authorities, especially in the primary grades, to set aside certain hours for talks on fire prevention, the safe way to cross streets, the use of the toothbrush, the duty of keeping the street clean, kindness to animals, the virtues of milk and spinach as contrasted with the vices of pastry and sweetmeats, and many other worthy but too numerous causes.[14]

Though educational standards and objectives continued to be debated on the national level and by the federal government, the major decisions and fundings were on the local level. The parents and citizens of the various states, counties, cities, and towns developed their own objectives for their schools.

Similar to many cities in the United States, by 1910, Boston had established an administrative structure to guide, regulate, and build schools. Unlike several European countries, a uniform national system dictating what each child studied from day to day did not become popular as a method for educational reform. In the United States, the independent spirit prevailed and local citizens of cities and towns formed school committees which were guided by state and county governments. Of course, Boston was a bit more complicated with the love of debate and politics adding zest to the system. As far back as 1647, the Commonwealth of Massachusetts regulated local education by requiring the establishment of schools, and Boston established its first Special Committee on Schools. From then until 1901, it ranged in membership from twenty-one to one hundred and sixteen people, and the school building departments were under the direction of the school committees. In 1901, the bureaucratic structure changed dramatically with the Commonwealth of Massachusetts legislative establishment of the Schoolhouse Department. By 1905, the legislature had reduced the School Committee to five members. Though the Schoolhouse Department turned the School Committee's programs into bricks and mortar, it was a strong bureaucratic entity. By 1910, the Schoolhouse Department was fully established and continued successfully for twenty-eight years until 1929 when the department was renamed and reorganized.

In 1915, the Panama-Pacific Exposition took place in San Francisco. Though far from Boston both physically and, perhaps, mentally, it reflected the attitudes of architects, educators, and citizens in general. Though America spanned a continent, lines of communication and travel tied it together. This was particularly true in architecture; in the spirit of architects from ancient Greece or the Italian renaissance, contemporary architects traveled for work and kept informed about architectural trends. The Panama-Pacific Exposition continued the classical revival style established by the 1893 Columbian Exposition in Chicago. However, the White City of Chicago had been transformed into the Jewel City of San Francisco. This California exposition burst forth with color in its buildings, flowers, and uniforms. There was an exuberant interpretation of the classical architectural style unknown twenty-two years before in Chicago. Education was featured among the exhibits. The Education Palace included information and examples for kindergartens, common schools, state agricultural colleges, industrial and vocational schools, and centralized urban schools. In addition to this, there were three model schools on site: a commercial business college, Palmer School of Penmanship, and Maria Montessori Preschool.[15] Both in architecture and education, there was an exploration that reflected back and forth across the nation.

The Boston public schools continued to be designed by noted local architects who created many other buildings that have become the backbone of our historic city. The firm of Brigham, Conveney &

Bisbee designed the Adams School in 1910; prior to that, Charles Brigham had designed the State House Rear Annex and the Christian Science Church. A.W. Longfellow, who received the commission for the large Boston High School of 1911, had previously completed the 1904 Fuller Mansion that is now part of Emerson College on Beacon Street. The 1911 Winthrop School was the beginning for Maginnis & Walsh when twenty-seven years later Charles D. Maginnis created the present chancel of Trinity Church in 1938. J.A. Schweinfurth, architect for the massive 1913 Dearborn Middle School and the smaller 1915 Dickerman School, had completed the 1904 New England College of Optometry in the French Style. Perhaps the most unusual firm was Blackall, Clapp and Whittemore headed by Clarence H. Blackall (1857–1942). Though architects for the 1919 R. Shaw Middle School, the firm specialized in theaters, including the 1900 Colonial Theater, the 1914 Wilbur Theater, and the 1925 Wang Center for the Performing Arts that form the theater district of Boston.[16]

The architects who designed schools and other buildings could receive their training in several ways. In the early United States, training was by apprenticeship in an architect's office. This apprenticeship training was a recognized method until well into the 1980s. The more acceptable and prestigious path was through organized classes. In 1830, Robert Mills established a school of architecture in Washington, D.C. About thirty-five years later the 1862 Morrill Land-Grant act brought forth a number of universities with architectural schools: the Massachusetts Institute of Technology in 1868, Cornell University in 1870, and University of Illinois in 1871. In 1911, there were twenty schools of architecture in the United States, and by law, the land-grant universities were open to both men and women.[17] However, since women were not particularly welcomed, the Cambridge School of Architecture and Landscape Architecture for women was founded in 1915 at Cambridge, Massachusetts. By 1919, there were a number of women architects practicing in Boston, but their male colleagues captured the commissions from the Schoolhouse Department. Before and after World War I, those who could afford it went to Paris to study at the École des Beaux Arts. Upon their return, they controlled the architectural schools and design attitudes. Consequently, there was an emphasis upon revivals of classical, gothic, and renaissance styles that dominated urban architecture in America.

The Boston Schoolhouse Department maintained high standards. They hired distinguished architects with varied experience in Boston; developed planning and construction methods that were incorporated into the buildings by the private architects; and cautiously accepted deviations from the classical revival style. With a few exceptions, such as the Dearborn Middle School, red brick dominated. Precast concrete was introduced to Boston at the 1911 Boston High School, originally named the Abraham Lincoln School. Metal stairways were embellished with rosettes, postcaps, and oak handrails. Oak bookcases and slate chalkboards were built into each classroom. With the intellectual upheavals of World War I, architects reinterpreted or moved away from the classical revival style, and the Boston School Department flowed with the professional tide. The schools before the war followed the classical style with decorative lintels, medallions, bands, and cornices. As time progressed, the interpretation became much freer with touches of gothic, moorish, and imagination. However, at most schools these stylistic changes were on the exterior wrapper that encapsulated the standard plans, finishes, and details developed by the Boston School-house Department.

The last annexation of neighboring towns was accomplished with the inclusion of Hyde Park in 1912, fixing the city's physical boundaries and commencing the process of growth and renewal within these boundaries. Boston's physical boundaries were fixed just as our nation's boundaries were fixed. Therefore, the city of Boston would become more urban as empty fields were filled with houses, shops, and schools. Boston had withstood the effects of World War I and the influenza epidemic. The flood of immigrants had been decreased. Industrialized New England needed skilled employees and the city planned and constructed schools to train these American workers. The war effort had formed a unified nation from disparate recent immigrants, but unfortunately this nation turned its back and closed the doors to others. America was for Americans.

FOOTNOTES

1. Slosson, Preston William, *The Great Crusade and After* 1914–1918, (New York, the MacMillan Company, 1930) p. 5.

2. Ibid, p. 25.

3. Ibid, p. 23.

4. Ibid, p. 12.

5. Russell, Francis, *The Great Interlude*, (New York, McGraw-Hill Book Company, 1964) p. 25.

6. Ibid, p. 92.

7. Slosson, Opis ibid, p. 299.

8. Schlereth, Thomas J., *Victorian America: Transformations in Everyday Life* 1876–1915, (New York, Harper Collins Publishers, 1991) p. 248.

9. Slosson, Opis ibid, p. 55.

10. Slosson, Opis ibid, p. 170.

11. *Encyclopaedia Britannica* (Chicago, Encyclopaedia Britannica, Inc., William Benton, Publishers, 1962) volume 20, pp. 257–259.

12. Ibid, p. 259.

13. Annual Reports of the Schoolhouse Department, City of Boston.

14. Slosson, Opis ibid, p. 326.

15. Schlereth, Opis ibid, p. 298.

16. Southworth, Susan and Michael, *The Boston Society of Architect's AIA Guide to Boston* (Chester, Connecticut, The Globe Pequot Press, 1992).

17. *Encyclopaedia Britannica*, Opis ibid, volume 2, p. 273.

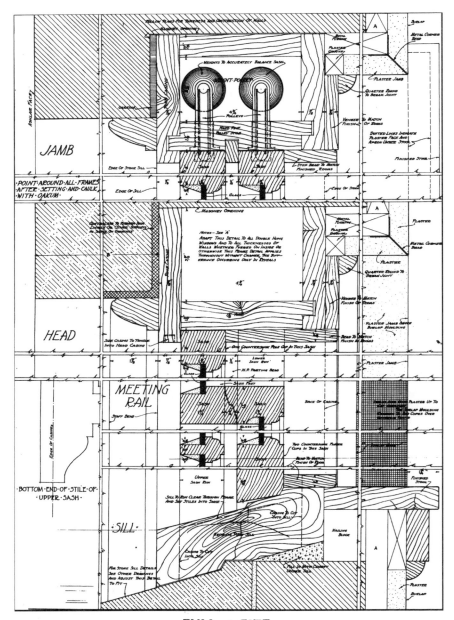

FULL · SIZE
DETAIL OF DOUBLE HUNG WINDOWS

Drawing of Window Details
Sarah Greenwood Elementary School
Dorchester, 1919

In 1919, the construction documents were drawn by hand; in 2002, they are drawn by computer. Though one hundred years have passed, the same graphic patterns are used for materials.

Drawing courtesy of Boston Public Schools, Campbell Center.

CHAPTER IV
The Roaring Twenties

With the end of World War 1, prosperity enveloped the United States and, along with it, the City of Boston. Prosperity brought increased opportunities for the children of the prewar immigrants, the hardworking poor, and the economically adventuresome. Though there was depression in 1920 and then inflation, the decade provided real economic gains for most Americans and certainly urban dwellers until the crash of 1929.[1] Business was venerated with both high schools and colleges providing commercial courses and business degrees.[2] However, economic opportunity for the majority did not translate into an understanding tolerance for the minority. Fear and suspicion of things different, foreign, or unknown swept through the populace. There were clashes between conservatives and liberals; adamant believers and questioning atheists; teatotalers and imbibers; fundamentalists and evolutionists; capitalists and workers; democrats and communists; intellectuals and pragmatists; established citizens and potential immigrants; liberated women and traditional males; and age and youth. Perceived improprieties in books, on stage, or in conduct were banned in Boston. It was a decade for the young at heart filled with opportunities, conflicts, challenges, extremes, adventure, sex, and money.

Immigration into the United States was severely restricted in the 1920s. The recent immigrants had become Americans and were uninterested in sharing or diluting their good fortune. Beginning in 1917 with a literacy requirement for immigrants, the gates were gradually closed. In 1921, annual immigration was limited to 3% of the resident nationals of the 1910 census.[3] A year later, the United States Supreme Court ruled that Japanese were not eligible for citizenship.[4] By 1924, the quota for immigrants was reduced to 2% based upon the 1890 census which, therefore, favored the British Isles and Germany; Japanese and Chinese immigrants were excluded, but Mexicans and Canadians could enter freely.[5] However, Massachusetts continued its interest in immigrants by establishment of a bureau in 1917 to help, protect, and promote assimilation. Restricted immigration changed the face of our nation and, consequently, the mission of urban public schools. No longer were there predominately foreign children to be assimilated and Americanized. Now the children were from American stock, and the goal was to form them into responsible and productive young adults.

The postwar economy brought change to Europe and America. Though Warren G. Harding had run and won the United States presidency in 1920 on a "back to normalcy" slogan, there was no back to normalcy for the European nations. The battles of the war had been fought upon European soil decimating the countryside, villages, and cities. The economic cost of the war had been tremendous for these nations; new concepts of government such as socialism and communism had gained strength; new nations had emerged; the balance of power had shifted away from Great Britain. For the United States, the changes were quite different. Since the battles had not been fought on our soil, our countryside, towns, and cities were left intact. However, there were economic consequences that would become more evident as the decade progressed. The United States had become a world power and now the European nations owed us money. Before World War I, the national debt was $1,188,235,400 in 1914, but in less than ten years the national debt had risen to $23,976,250,608 in 1921. Due to wartime demands, factory capacity and agricultural production had been expanded beyond peacetime needs. Thus, our economic structure was off balance causing workers' strikes (such as the Boston police strike), buyers' strike, and the 1920 depression which was soon followed by inflation. It was the inflation that created new poor as well as new rich. People on fixed incomes such as government employees, school teachers, and college professors found themselves in reduced economic circumstances. Meanwhile, workers with rising wages and businessmen with land and goods profited from rising prices to become the new rich.[6]

The intellectual liberals defied the pragmatic conservatives in their writings, attitudes, morals, and conduct. Frederick Lewis Allen, an author of the period, defined the credo of the intellectuals in his book *Only Yesterday: An Informed History of the Nineteen-Twenties* that included seven major points.

1. Practice sexual freedom
2. Defy blue laws
3. Antiprohibitionists
4. Religious skepticism
5. Scorn of bourgeois majority
6. Overturn idols of the majority
7. Against American mass production

Not to be outdone, Malcolm Cowley in *Exile's Return* summarized the bohemian intellectuals' viewpoint with eight points: the idea of salvation by the child; self expression; paganism (enjoyment of the body); living for the moment; liberty; female equality; psychological adjustment; and changing place (expatriates). It was the "lost generation" with the romance of F. Scott Fitzgerald and the pathos of John Dos Passos. For some people, the intellectuals' credo translated into a free lifestyle, and for others it became a topic for thoughtful reflection, but in Boston the reaction was often different.

> *In Boston, where they were backed by an alliance between stubborn Puritanism and Roman Catholicism, they banned books wholesale, forbade the stage presentation of* Strange Interlude, *and secured the conviction of a bookseller for selling* Lady Chatterly's Lover—*only to find that the intellectuals of the whole country were laughing at them . . .*[7]

The conservative majority was at times intolerant and restrictive. By 1920, the political revolutions of Europe had created a "Red Scare" in the United States with a fear that the Bolsheviks were trying to take over the country. Suspicions of radicalism were not tolerated and school teachers were asked to sign oaths of allegiance.[8] Boston joined in this hysteria with the arrest of Sacco and Vanzetti in 1920 and their execution in 1927.[9] The Ku Klux Klan found renewed strength in the south playing on extreme nationalism and racial prejudice.[10] The desire to regulate everyone transformed the wartime liquor prohibition to national prohibition in 1920 creating a market for bootleg liquor and speakeasies. Intolerance could take the form of hatred against African-Americans, Jews, and Roman Catholics.[11] Some Boston school students were not immune to these feelings though the teachers did not condone intolerance. Francis Russell expressed his teenage hatreds as a white, middle-class protestant youth in *The Great Interlude* written many years later in 1964 with startling candor.

> *In my day, the majority of the Boston Latin [School] students were Jewish . . . I hated the Boston Latin School as an impersonal prison of*

the mind, and on my first intimate contact I disliked Jews . . . Taken from my friends at Roxbury [Latin School], suddenly thrust into a crowd of pushing little Jews, I was aware only of their unpleasantness, knowing nothing of the relentless, grinding processes that had made them so different from the boys I had known.[12]

The "Younger Generation" was considered a problem by their elders. Young people seemed disillusioned, wanted a good time, and were tired of restrictions. Women bobbed their hair, rolled down their stockings, wore short dresses, smoked cigarettes, and sought independence. Ballroom dancing was not only cheek-to-cheek but also body-to-body. High schoolers were reportedly going to petting parties. Sex was on peoples minds and in books, plays, and movies. This was declared the decade of "Bad Manners" as men and women drank, smoked, and swore together. The radio spread news and entertainment across rural America and with it urban tastes. Closed cars provided privacy to courting couples away from prying eyes in the family parlor. By 1928, the quest for independence had increased the divorce rate to one for every six marriages.[13] Young people in high schools and colleges might not have understood the intellectuals, but they felt they could do as they pleased as long as it did no harm to others. To rise from poverty to wealth, from dependence to independence were the goals.[14] Success in business could support these good times and education could provide the training for success.

The demands of business for skilled and literate workers affected the curriculum and attendance at schools. In 1914, unskilled labor dominated, but by 1926, skilled and unskilled labor were about equal. The 1920 census recorded decreases in the farm population, particularly in New England, and a movement towards the industrialized towns.[15] With business booming, more jobs were open to women, and they gladly expanded into publishing, advertising, real estate, shop management, and department- store buyers.[16] These economic pressures and opportunities made secondary education essential for young people to succeed in the business world. Therefore, enrollment in secondary schools increased to 50% of all high school age children by 1927. With this, the number of school days increased and attendance also went up.[17] Though academic courses continued, vocational training became popular for boys with various machine, printing, and woodworking shops. For the girls, domestic science dominated with cooking, sewing, millinery, and household management. Office training was also available with courses in typing, stenography, and accounting at the high school level. With this combination of academic and vocational courses, high school graduates were prepared to join the thriving American workforce.

The battle between religion and science extended into the classroom. The fundamentalists with an unbending interpretation of the bible brought John Thomas Scopes, a public high school teacher, to trial for teaching evolution. Though this 1925 case in Tennessee was a sensation throughout the country, it had little effect upon the general reliance for science and technology to explain our world and solve our problems. Albert Einstein was already a world-famous scientist for his theory of relativity when he visited this country in 1921 and was greeted as a celebrity by the mayor of New York City. To encourage this belief in science, by 1921, the Science Service had been founded in Washington D.C., with the goal of making science more understandable to the general public.[18] In the high schools, the public interest was transformed into courses in mathematics, science, and technology. Though mathematics could be taught in a standard classroom, science produced extensive laboratories for instruction and experimentation and, of course, technology demanded well-equipped shops. Though some ministers were preaching hell, fire, and damnation, the public educators and business leaders had faith in science and technology to better mankind's fate, at least on earth.

Expanded interests and leisure time for adults influenced the range of activities in the schools. For example, sports became very popular in the 1920s for both participants and observers. The recently liberated woman swam the English Channel, flew planes, and played basketball and golf along with her male colleagues. College football and local baseball games were among the many spectator sports. All of this interest led to increased physical exercise and training in schools and, therefore, gymnasia were constructed for new schools and added to existing schools. The public's fascination with movies and continued delight in vaudeville and theater intensified with more leisure time, income, and education. Some of this interest in theater was reflected in high school facilities funded in the 1920s. Large assembly halls were usually included for high schools and often for elementary schools that provided a stage for theatricals and a projection booth for motion pictures. Eating became more than a way to satisfy hunger, but a means to increase health and demonstrate manners for the new middle class. This interest in nutrition, along with the lengthened school day and larger school districts, produced the high school cafeteria serving lunches as well as domestic science suites emphasizing genteel manners. As usual, the public expected the schools to prepare its students for various aspects of the contemporary American life.

To Americans, education was more than learning the basic ABCs; it was society's opportunity to mold, influence, and even indoctrinate young people. What political and social views were to be advocated was the question in the 1920s as in other decades. The experiences of World War I had disillusioned the young and strengthened antiwar sentiment. War was no longer romanticized by novelists or journalists. Public school history text books were reviewed and criticized for glorifying war.[19] President Wilson's dream for the League of Nations was out of favor as the opposition gathered around their leader, Henry Cabot Lodge, United States Senator from Massachusetts.[20] Though many intellectuals still looked to Europe for cultural standards, even they were beginning to admire American literature, theater, and thoughts. However, for some, an increased sense of national pride developed into isolationism. While all these issues and others were debated, there appeared to be a consensus that it was appropriate to include such issues in the educational agenda.

> But this belief that the schools had a primary responsibility towards peace was widely and sincerely shared by members of the educational establishment, who thus carried to its zenith the familiar American gospel that there is no goal, from universal affluence to racial justice, that a well-financed public school system cannot accomplish.[21]

In Boston, there was disagreement concerning technical education, class sizes, expenditures, and portable classrooms. The Boston Schoolhouse Department in its 1929 final report lamented waste and delays, the expenditure of school funds for a swimming pool and a community library.

Schools have been built for high and intermediate purposes which have been used for intermediate and elementary grades; sites have been taken; plans prepared and even bids received for school buildings, only to have the projects abandoned or indefinitely postponed; plans have been revised before and after advertising for bids; fundamental changes in buildings under construction have been made; and drastic changes in new buildings after completion have been effected, all as a result of written requests of the Superintendent of Schools, on the ground of educational needs.

These, apart from the serious delays involved, have resulted in the wasteful expenditure of large sums of money, all, with exception of certain land takings, during the past four years.[22]

The Board of the Schoolhouse Department grumbled on with their complaints of spending too much money on shops and machinery, though they did acknowledge the School Committee's responsibility to determine the value of industrial education. According to the Schoolhouse Commissioners, too many shops and underutilization of space caused overuse of portable classrooms. The Board suggested an increase to 40 pupils in each classroom; decried the use of a classroom as a teachers' room; and recommended a sewing class be moved to a rarely used auditorium. Advocating a change in policy, the Schoolhouse Department complained that the number of portable classrooms had remained the same though there had been a net gain of 11,905 permanent seats in the system. The report did verify that Boston followed national trends with more students staying for longer periods of time in high schools and intermediate schools. To meet this increased demand, seven high schools and eight intermediate schools had been constructed during their four-year regime 1925–1929. With these schools came "numerous auditoria, gymnasia, shops of all kinds, lunchrooms, laboratory and science rooms, libraries, and a swimming pool." Though critical and outspoken in their final report, they proudly noted "that no section of the city has been overlooked in the program to provide suitable accommodations for the school children."[23]

By 1920, Boston had developed very specific design guidelines for its schools that were revised periodically through 1929. The Appendix VI General Information As To Standard Requirements For School

Buildings and Yards filled sixty-one pages with directions from play yards to vacuum cleaner systems. Little was left to chance or the imagination for lower elementary, upper elementary, and junior high schools. Detailed directions were provided for schoolrooms, fresh-air rooms, wardrobes, corridors and vestibules, staircases, sanitaries, playrooms, master's and teachers' rooms, assembly halls, manual training rooms, cooking room, sewing room, and nurse's room. High schools had their own detailed criteria for chemistry, chemical laboratory, lecture and recitation room, administrative facilities, physical laboratory, apparatus rooms, botanical and zoological laboratory, gymnasium and drill hall, manual arts room, household science, lunchrooms, library, wardrobes, and electric work. An example of the level of detail can be seen in the schoolroom requirements that covered ten topics.

1. Size
2. Windows
3. Doors
4. Floors
5. Walls
6. Ceilings
7. Artificial Light
8. Heating and Ventilation
9. Bookcase
10. Teacher's Closet

The size of the classroom was to be "23 by 29 for lower and upper elementary grades, 26 by 32 for junior high, and not less than 12 feet high in clear." Windows were to be "on the long side for left-hand lighting." The glass measured inside the sash was to "contain not less than one-fifth of floor area." Doors were to be "3 feet 6 inches by 7 feet, partly glazed to open out, placed preferably near the teacher's end . . . [with] brass- plated, ball-bearing steel butts, 4-lever mortise lock, master keyed; cast brass knob, flush marble thresholds to corridors for first-class construction." The instructions went on and on giving the preferred color for upper plaster walls—"a warm grey green or buff gives the best results"—the number of pendent mounted ceiling lights, the types of pulls on bookcase drawers—"small brass pull."[24] It was a remarkable collection of advice representing years of experience that had been codified in the 1920s to produce building design standards that would be used throughout the 1920s and 1930s until World War II stopped all new construction.

The architecture of the 1920s was an eclectic array of various styles in the United States and particularly in Boston. Classical, Gothic, Romanesque, Spanish, and the Unnamed were combined to produce homes, banks, office buildings, universities, and schools. It was an age of opulence that could afford the costly decoration of these historic styles. Even in the construction budgets of Boston public schools, there was money for elaborately carved stone medallions, garlands, turrets, quoins, lintels, cornices, and pilasters. Boston continued using historic forms throughout the 1920s. However, there were signs of a new architecture that cast off the historic styles of Europe. This international modernism was championed by such architects as Le Corbusier in France, Gropius in Germany, and Wright in Chicago. These modern architects stripped away historic decoration and began to develop a new esthetic for contemporary materials, life-styles, and building types such as skyscrapers. By 1925, there were 1,600 buildings in New York City with more than ten stories.[25] Meanwhile, educational buildings would continue to be clad in the historic while internally the schools were designed for the modern scientific, technical, and industrial teaching facilities.

The architects selected to design the Boston public schools were established in their profession and leaders in their community. William W. Drummey, who designed the Beethoven Elementary School in 1925, went on to create the modern style Conley School in 1931, to become the Superintendent of Construction for the City of Boston, and later to found the architectural firm of Drummey Rosane Anderson Inc. (DRA) that still specialized in schools in 2001. Parker, Thomas & Rice, architects for the 1909 Hale School and the 1923 McKinley School, have been credited with the first skyscraper in Boston—1928 Art Deco United Shoe Machinery Building on High Street in downtown Boston.[26] Many of the architects who had designed Boston schools in the past would continue designing Boston schools in the future. Architectural firms such as Harrison H. Attwood, William W. Drummey, and John M. Gray would provide continuity of design through several decades. Consequently, the Schoolhouse Department's design guidelines, construction details, and building materials were easily standardized throughout the school system.

In 1929, the stock market crashed. Though it recovered slightly, the decade of prosperity was finished. The volatility of the 1920s, its conflicts, challenges, and adventure had irrevocably changed the social, political, and educational patterns in the United States. There was no turning back for the middle and lower economic classes who had seen opportunities expand through education. This decade had demonstrated that with favorable circumstances, education, and hard work the poor could become rich, the downtrodden could become powerful. Though the following decade would be economically depressed, the distant roar of the twenties could be heard: remember, education is the key to your future success.

FOOTNOTES

1. Slosson, Preston William, *The Great Crusade and After* 1914–1918 (New York, The MacMillan Company, 1930) p. 420.

2. Allen, Frederick Lewis, *Only Yesterday: An Informal History of the Nineteen-Twenties* (New York, Harper 4 Brothers Publishers, 1931) p. 177.

3. Slosson, Opus ibid, p. 299.

4. Sullivan, Mark, *Our Times, The United States* 1900–1925, VI *The Twenties* (New York, Charles Scribner's Sons, 1935) p. 582.

5. Slosson, Opus ibid, p. 300.

6. Sullivan, Opus ibid, pp. 1–13.

7. Allen, Opus ibid, p. 114.

8. Allen, Opus ibid, p. 58.

9. Boylan, James editor, *The World of the 20s*, p. 136.

10. Sullivan, Opus ibid, p. 543.

11. Allen, Opus ibid, p. 62.

12. Russell, Francis, *The Great Interlude* (New York, McGraw-Hill Book Company, 1964) pp. 103, 104, 105.

13. Allen, Opus ibid, pp. 88–116.

14. Sullivan, Opus ibid, pp. 396, 435.

15. Slosson, Opus ibid, pp. 301, 197.

16. Allen, Opus ibid, p. 97.

17. Slosson, Opus ibid, pp. 320, 322.

18. Carter, Paul A., *Another Part of the Twenties* (New York, Columbia University Press, 1977) pp. 63–73.

19. Carter, Opus ibid, p. 36.

20. Allen, Opus ibid, p. 28.

21. Carter, Opus ibid, p. 36.

22. *Annual Report of the Schoolhouse Department for Twelve Months Ending December 30, 1929* (City of Boston Printing Department, 1930) p. 3.

23. *Annual Report*, Opus ibid, pp. 2, 3.

24. *Annual Report of the Schoolhouse Department from February 1, 1919, to February 1, 1920*, Appendix VI General Information as to Standard Requirements for School Buildings and Yards, (City of Boston Printing Department, 1920).

25. Slosson, Opus ibid, p. 48.

26. Southworth, Susan and Michael, *The Boston Society of Architect's AIA Guide to Boston* (Chester, Connecticut, The Globe Pequot Press, 1992).

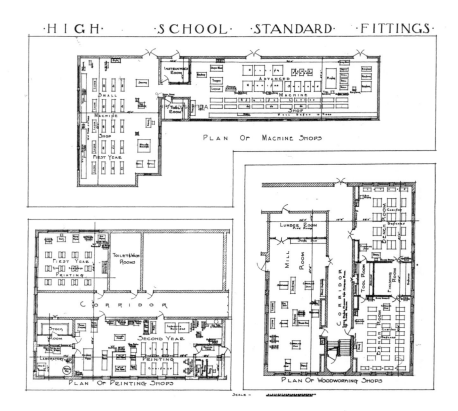

PLAN OF MACHINE SHOPS

PLAN OF PRINTING SHOPS

PLAN OF WOODWORKING SHOPS

High School Standard Fittings
Annual Report of the Schoolhouse Department
January 1, 1929, to December 31, 1929

These prototypical plans illustrated the growing interest in vocational and practical training for high school students. More young people wanted to complete their secondary education, and their goal was to be trained for the industrialized economy. The Standard Fittings had floor plans for the machine, printing, woodworking shops, and mechanical drawing room. These spaces were well equipped with machinery and tools related to the various trades. The training in these shops combined with the academic courses prepared the students to be productive employees. *Illustrations courtesy of Boston Public Schools.*

CHAPTER V

A New Deal

THE 1930S WITH THE GREAT DEPRESSION WAS A PERIOD OF enormous hardship for people in Boston, throughout the United States, and most of the world. It began with the stock market crash of 1929 and lasted until our country entered World War II in 1941. Then our nation's attention was focused upon another difficult four years as we fought our way successfully through a great war and out of the Great Depression. The economic hardships affected all aspects of our lives, our hearts, and our minds. The daily activities of adults and school children were changed due to lack of available jobs and, consequently, a shortage of money for food, clothing, housing, and recreation. Though the Great Depression certainly did not diminish people's propensity for falling in and out of love, it did discourage young couples from having children and, therefore, the birthrate dropped as people realized that they could not afford the cost of raising and educating more children.[1] Remarkably, our minds were able to withstand the shock of the economic calamity beginning with the crash of 1929 and continuing with subsequent shocks through the years of banks closed, homes lost, savings gone, careers ruined, and jobs terminated. Perhaps because our world (or our idealized concept of our world) was turned upside down and was torn apart by the effects of the Great Depression, people looked to new ideas, new methods, new politics, new education, new architecture, and the New Deal offered by the new president, Franklin D. Roosevelt, in 1933 to get us out of this mess.

The economic conditions of the 1930s might have been too reminiscent of the Old World left behind. Though the Immigration Act of 1924 had reduced the flow of immigrants, the Boston population of 781,000 included more than 50% foreign-born in 1930. (Boston was similar to the seventeen other cities with over 250,000 people in these population statistics.)[2] By 1930, the original Yankee settlers had moved to the suburbs being supplanted by the Irish with a mixture of Italians, Jews, and other European groups. The city was three-quarters Catholic, the Irish were strong in the labor unions and firmly established in city government. However, the minds and souls of these various ethnic groups were similar in that they could remember why they had come to this country. They and their ancestors certainly had not made the long voyage to continue the old life of economic and social deprivation. The situation was becoming so desperate that even Bostonians were willing to try new ways, though tempered by the political twists and social turns of the Hub.

As the decade progressed, the economic situation deteriorated gradually until the nation, and Boston, came to realize that the economy was not going to right itself without drastic measures by the government. In Massachusetts, the industrial labor force dropped from 650,000 in 1920 to 481,000 in 1930; the unemployment figure for all trades rose to an alarming 30% in 1932.[3] However, Boston was not fully in control of its own destiny to attempt an economic cure. Due to previous political shenanigans, the City of Boston government was regulated by the state government and could not raise its taxes or its debt level without state approval. When James Michael Curley took office in January 1930 for his third term as Mayor of Boston, he proudly announced his "Fifty-Year Plan" filled with public construction projects to get the city's economy moving forward. But he had little success in convincing Governor Joseph B. Ely to approve the required construction loans and did no better on the federal level with President Hoover. All of these grand plans were to wait until after Roosevelt became president in 1933, Mansfield became mayor in 1934, and Curley became governor of Massachusetts.

The situation with the Boston public schools was better. Though the state regulated the city government and set the school budget, the citizens of Boston elected the School Committee which still had the power to determine the budget for the construction and repair of school buildings. With 145,000 school children in 1931 (as compared to 63,000 in 1999) there continued to be a need for new schools. Though the birthrate was dropping and affected elementary schools, the demand for high schools and middle schools increased. Parents, educators, and politicians were in agreement that increased education, the completion of a full high school curriculum, was essential for young people to overcome the challenges of the depression years. There were twenty-two schools completed from 1930 through 1939, which were still used as active public schools nearly sixty years later in 2001. The Boston School Committee and the Schoolhouse Department continued to construct, plan, and design contemporary and visionary learning environments for the children of Boston in spite of limited support from state and federal administrations.

President Roosevelt's New Deal, and particularly the Public Works Administration (PWA), had an enormous effect upon the design and construction of schools across the nation. However, PWA funding was not fully implemented until 1936. This, along with Boston's penchant for political squabbles and fiscal conservatism brought less federal PWA money to Boston than might be expected. Boston received no PWA money until 1935 and then the amount was only $679,504. At that time, the federal government paid 30% towards the cost of labor and materials and the other 70% had to be covered by municipal bonds. This improved significantly in 1936 with the federal government increasing its contribution to 45% of the total cost of the project, thereby reducing the municipal cost to 55% for a project. However, the Boston business leaders were not pleased with the city's debt increases to meet PWA funding requirements; the city's trade unions wanted to control the PWA labor force; and the politicians wanted the distribution of projects to bolster their political support. Finally in 1936–37, Boston received $3,549,000 from PWA and the city financed $8,700,000 in municipal bonds. Five schools constructed with PWA funds continued in 2001 to be used successfully as active public schools in Boston.

The PWA was only one of many programs devised by President Roosevelt and his administration. The alphabet was mixed and shaken to form the Civilian Conservation Corps (CCC); Civil Works Administration (CWA); Federal Emergency Relief Administration (FERA); Massachusetts Emergency Relief Administration (MERA); National Industrial Recovery Act (NIRA); National Recovery Administration (NRA); Works Progress Administration (WPA), and many others too numerous to remember or mention. However, of this vast array of alphabet soup, PWA and WPA were the most influential in architecture and the arts. Before WPA there was the Public Works of Art Project (PWAP), which hired painters and sculptors to decorate public buildings. WPA was much more inclusive and provided all sorts of work for needy people. Within WPA, there was the Federal project #1 for art, music, theater and writers' projects. WPA artists completed about 2,500 murals and 18,000 pieces of sculpture nationwide.[4] Several of these murals and other works of art brought graceful beauty to the Boston public schools.

With PWA funding came procedures, reviews, and suggestions by the federal administrators. The regional PWA administration was divided into three branches: engineering, legal, and financial. The PWA engineer would help the town or city fill out the application form, but the local architect would provide the design and construction drawings. The U.S. Division of Information proudly reported that "nearly 6,000 engineering and architectural firms and individuals have participated in the program."[5]

In general, matters of design were left to the local communities, but the federal government did have defined projects that they considered fundable.

> In general, PWA allotments for school construction have served four main purposes: (1) To provide new facilities to meet the needs of shifting populations and growing enrollments; (2) to replace unsafe and obsolete small buildings with modern, consolidated schools; (3) to provide new structures with modern equipment to replace obsolete and overcrowded buildings without proper heating, ventilation, lighting, or sanitation; and (4) to provide needed additions and improvements to existing buildings.[6]

What did this mean for school buildings? Two out of every five schools had been built before the turn of the century (maybe 40 years old in 1935); the federal government deemed most of these to be obsolete and encouraged demolition and replacement. There were still a number of one-room schoolhouses with ungraded classes; the federal government encouraged the consolidation of school districts by providing funding towards the construction of 791 new consolidated schools and the demolition of 1,582 smaller schools throughout rural America. The high school population had more than doubled since 1920, creating multiple sessions in urban areas; the federal government redefined the modern high school education and the facilities to be provided. No longer were basic classrooms sufficient; now the high schools were to include laboratories, shops, auditoria, gymnasia, libraries, cafeterias, study halls, and science and commercial classrooms. Facilities for technical training were to be provided so that young people could learn to make a living in business and industry: typewriting, bricklaying, farming, and engineering needed special facilities. Electrical shops, auto shops, manual-training shops, and domestic-science shops were to be pro-

Front Facade, Margaret Fuller Elementary, Jamaica Plain, 1892
This is the oldest school building that continues to be used as a school in Boston. (*Photograph by Nick Wheeler*)

Entry Facade, F. Lyman Winship Elementary School, Brighton, 1901
Red brick and decorative limestone trim were combined to create lively facades at historic Boston schools. (*Photograph by Nick Wheeler*)

Assembly Hall, Thomas Gardner Elementary School, Allston, 1906
The decorative classical plaster frieze was filled with lively horses and riders
galloping around the perimeter. (*Photograph by Richard Mandelkorn*)

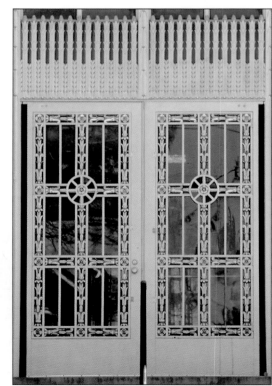

**Entry Doors
Thomas A. Edison
Middle School
Brighton, 1932**
The artistry of this door
grille combined several
principles of the 1930s
modern architecture.
(*Photograph by Nick Wheeler*)

Auditorium Overview, Jeremiah Burke High School, Dorchester, 1934
The first high school in Boston to be designed in the style of modern
architecture used new materials and abstract decorations.
(Photograph by Nick Wheeler)

**Stair Hall Detail
Patrick F. Gavin
Middle School
South Boston, 1936**
The green and black
vitrolite wall panels were
designed and installed as
part of the WPA artists
program.
(Photograph by Nick Wheeler)

Class Gift
Jeremiah E. Burke
High School
Dorchester, 1946

The women on the WWII Honor Roll remind us that the Jeremiah Burke School was a high school for girls until the 1970s.

(*Photograph by Nick Wheeler*)

Exterior Facade, Madison Park High School, Roxbury, 1978
The design for the campus high school abandoned the traditional red brick and replaced it with grey concrete.

(*Photograph by Nick Wheeler*)

vided for the modern education. These were the standards of the federal government and were applied to school projects receiving PWA assistance. Also these standards reflected the attitudes of educators and permeated the educational systems whether or not receiving financial aid.

Many of these educational standards had been adopted, developed, and refined by the Boston Schoolhouse Department long before the 1930s and incorporated into Boston's school buildings. Some had been rejected and some had been modified to suit Boston's vision for its young people. Boston tempered the federal government's more blanket rejection of old schools. Since the city received less PWA money, it was subjected to fewer federal standards. Perhaps it was Boston's fiscal conservatism and political squabbles that unwittingly preserved some of its historic schools, though adapting them to the new standards. With good reason, the spirit of the 1930s and the New Deal looked ahead to the new rather than back to the old. This hope for the future and belief in new ideas pervaded literature, art, and architecture as well as education, politics, and social programs.

A new deal brought a new architecture. Modern architecture essentially began in the 1930s as architects looked for a new vocabulary to express contemporary life and the potential of manufactured materials. Modern architecture abandoned the classical vocabulary of fluted columns, carved bases and capitals, cornices trimmed with dentils or darts and arrows, and friezes and pediments decorated with carvings of mythological gods and goddesses. The new architecture stripped away this classical decoration to reveal the simple strong lines of composition, volumes, and massing accented by geometric motifs. Classical architecture was often associated with the old stratified world order of kings and queens, rich and poor, and haves and have-nots; it was a world shaken by World War I, challenged in the 1920s, and collapsing in the 1930s. Modern architecture strove to express the potential and hope for a new world order of political, economic, and intellectual exploration and change; it was a future for governments representing the will of the common people, for industry supporting the needs of working families, and for artists expressing the goals of the new social order. The industrial age had been embraced and industrial materials were lauded. Steel, glass, aluminum, concrete, and vitrolite were among the materials, and buildings became machines for living. The new aesthetic emphasized the expression of materials and construction methods. The plans and facades were to express the function and activities within the building. Decoration grew from the materials, function, and construction/manufacturing process. Along with this social idealism and industrial advancement came the harsh realities of the Great Depression. The economic restrictions encouraged the limited decoration and the clean lines of modern architecture.

The roots of modern architecture were in the earlier movements of the nineteenth century. Both in Europe and the United States architects continuously explored the potential for architecture to serve current needs and break from classicism. Various styles of architecture, along with innovations in structural engineering, were applied to new and ongoing building types. In England, Ruskin followed the mediaeval style while Morris (1834–1896) advocated the arts and crafts movement. In France, Viollet-le-Duc (1814–1879) reinterpreted gothic architecture as structure and Eiffel designed the framework of the remarkable Eiffel Tower (1887). In Massachusetts, Henry Hobson Richardson (1838–86) selected the romanesque style for Trinity Church in Boston and for a series of small public libraries and suburban train stations. The classicists centered around the École des Beaux Arts in Paris responded to these rebellions with innovative plans, facades, and details. The century progressed with the Gothic style becoming popular for colleges, churches, and schools as exemplified by Ralph Adams Cram (1863–1942) in the United States. The departure from classicism continued with the art nouveau movement represented by the art school building in Glasgow, Scotland, designed by Mackintosh (1898), the cathedral and park in Barcelona, Spain, designed by Gaudi (1852–1926) and, of course, the well-known lamps and interiors designed by Louis Comfort Tiffany in the United States. However, the deepest and most important root for modern architecture was in Chicago with a decidedly new building type, the skyscraper, in the 1890s. The invention of the elevator and the development of metal-frame buildings allowed this new building type to expand and with it modern architecture began its rise towards prominence.

Modern architecture was an international movement of the twentieth century with many branches and interpretations. In Germany and

Austria of the 1900s there were groups of architects moving towards modern architecture. Three young architects—Le Corbusier, Gropius, and Mies Van der Rohe—who worked in Peter Behren's office would go on as visible proponents of the modern movement. Le Corbusier was to publish his treatise *Vers une Architecture* in 1923; Gropius designed his model factory in Cologne in 1914 and assumed the directorship of the design school in Weimar in 1919 that was to become the Bauhaus in Dessau in 1924. It was here at the Bauhaus that modern architecture most strongly preached its philosophy and aesthetic. Mies Van der Rohe succeeded Gropius at the Bauhaus in 1930 after completing his enormously successful German pavilion for the international exposition in Barcelona of 1929. The modern movement was presented in Finland by the Helsinki railroad station (1910–1914) of Eliel Saarinen and spread through Europe in the early 1930s touching Switzerland, Finland, Sweden, England, Russia, Mexico, and South America.

This modern movement was known to architects in the United States and developed by many with various interpretations. Chicago continued to be central to modern architecture in the United States as the first home of the skyscraper. When tall buildings began to pop up in New York, Philadelphia, and other larger cities, modern methods were refined and utilized to construct and clad these buildings. Another branch of modern architecture in Chicago was represented by the independent Frank Lloyd Wright (1869–1959) with his prairie architecture used primarily for houses. His book of drawings—many of which were actually done by architect Marion Mahoney Griffin (1871–1961)—was published in Berlin in 1910 and influenced the movement in Germany and Finland.[7] This cross fertilization continued among architects. For example, Boston architect Eleanor Raymond traveled to Germany in the late 1920s and promptly returned to produce the 1931 house in Belmont, Massachusetts, with her interpretation of modern architecture. In 1932, the public was introduced to modern architecture, now called the International Style, at the Museum of Modern Art in New York City, and Rockefeller Center was begun in 1931. With the rise of Hitler, by 1935 many architects were forced to leave Germany and other countries. They came to the United States bringing with them a devotion to modern architecture.

When Gropius arrived in Boston in 1937, he was greeted by a

knowledgeable group of colleagues. Though many architects continued in the classical tradition, the inherent simplicity of New England buildings tempered all architectural styles. President Roosevelt's New Deal was in full swing, PWA was generously funded, and even Boston had received federal construction money. Architect Eleanor Raymond had completed the house in Belmont, Massachusetts, in 1931 and had also completed the sculptor's studio in Dover, Massachusetts, in 1933, both in the modern international style. Eleanor Manning O'Connor, along with a team of other architects, had completed the complex of buildings for the first low income public housing in Boston in 1937 that combined the new architecture with New England traditions. The Boston Department of School Buildings and their private architects had joined the group of modernists with the Conley Elementary School in Roslindale (1931), the Edison Middle School in Brighton (1932), and the Jeremiah Burke High School in Dorchester (1934). All of these buildings in the modern style had a distinctly Boston accent. The stark white walls and horizontal strip windows of German architecture were gone. The Bostonian's fondness for red brick, double-hung windows, wood houses, and garden courtyards prevailed.

Modern architecture moved out to Hollywood and into the movies flickering back across the nation and, of course, to the theaters of Boston. It was not an esoteric style just for the intellectuals and socially elite. Fred Astaire danced his way through and around decidedly sleek and modern sets; he bounced lightly onto modern tables; and twirled his partners up shining ramps. He, in his white tie and tails, and the woman, in her filmy gown, were smiling, scheming, and getting the best of the world. Comedians like the Marx brothers were helping to make people laugh in spite of the deep depression woes. The Marx brothers were roller skating through the new department store, getting folded up in the Murphy beds that looked like refrigerators and squeezed into refrigerators that looked like beds. It was a topsy-turvy world, but all in good fun where the little guy came out on top. It was the New-World Order coming true—at least in the movies.

Unfortunately, there were other connotations and associations which developed around modern architecture. It was used by some to support deplorable actions; it represented a radically new social order for others; and it just plain frightened a few. As Germany came under the spell of Hitler and the Nazis, many architects who supported modernism in architecture were forced to flee, but of course, some modernists remained. The simplicity of modern architecture and the motifs of classical Greece were combined by Hitler's favorite architect, Albert Speer, to create the neoclassical style.[8] This style was used by Speer to design dramatic sets for Hitler's political rallies and to clad government buildings in monumental grandeur. Both in Nazi Germany and Fascist Italy, the simplicity of modern architecture was transformed into an austere monumental architecture that Americans found repugnant as World War II came closer. In the Soviet Union, the communist revolutionaries embraced a form of modern architecture to express their New-World Order empowering the workers and challenging the capitalists, but this eventually changed as Stalin took control. In the United States, modern architecture survived along with its architects, engineers, and contractors. However, the WPA artists and writers were scrutinized and investigated by the United States Congress House Committee on un-American activities in 1938. Headed by Texas Democrat, Martin Dies, the committee held hearings to search out radicals and communists who might be lurking behind the murals, posters, or guidebooks produced by WPA artists.[9] These associations with political forms far removed from the basic ideals of modern architecture have perhaps at times clouded opinions of this architecture and its philosophy.

The PWA federal funding of school construction continued through the decade of the 1930s until the United States entered World War II in 1941. In 1937, the PWA Extension Act appropriated money and required that as of July 1, 1939 the projects be completed and PWA staff terminated.[10] This was later extended to June 30, 1940. The WPA programs for the arts were merged into the graphics section of the war services program in 1942 and by 1943 the arts program had stopped. The United States was officially out of the Great Depression, but was now into World War II for another brutal four years. Young men and women, often recent graduates from those new PWA schools, were sent off to fight. Mothers went to factories, fathers went to war, and families were split. The idealism of modern architecture faced the realities of modern warfare. All school construction stopped in Boston.

FOOTNOTES

1. United States Division of Information, *America Builds, The Record of the* PWA (Washington, United States Printing Office, 1939) p. 132.

2. Trout, Charles H., Boston, *The Great Depression and the New Deal* (New York, Oxford University Press, 1977).

3. Ibid.

4. Meltzer, Milton, *Violins & Shovels, The* WPA *Arts Projects* (New York, Delacorte Press, 1976).

5. United States Division of Information, op. cit., Chapter VI.

6. Ibid, p. 128.

7. Torre, Susana (Ed.), *Women in American Architecture*: A *Historic and Contemporary Perspective* (New York, Whitney Library of Design, 1977).

8. Speer, Albert, *Inside the Third Reich*, (New York, Avon Books, 1971) p. 101.

9. Meltzer, op. cit.

10. United States Division of Information , op. cit.

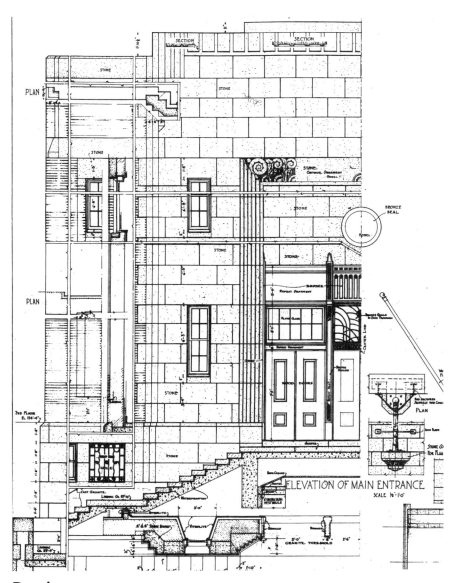

ELEVATION OF MAIN ENTRANCE
SCALE ½"=1'0"

Drawing
Martin Luther King Jr. Middle School
Dorchester, 1937

This drawing was one of many produced by the architect, Funk &
Wilcox, to explain how the building was to be constructed. Drawn by
hand with ink and pencil on a coated linen sheet, it was a durable
document, which has lasted more than half a century. On this drawing, the architect illustrated the exterior of the school auditorium.

Drawing courtesy of Boston Public Schools, Campbell Center.

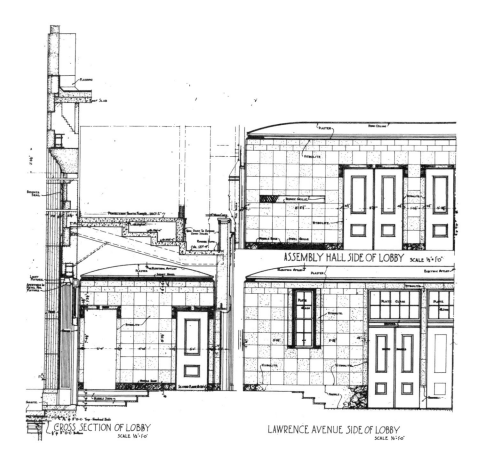

ASSEMBLY HALL SIDE OF LOBBY SCALE ½"=1'0"

CROSS SECTION OF LOBBY
SCALE ½"=1'0"

LAWRENCE AVENUE SIDE OF LOBBY
SCALE ½"=1'0"

Drawing
Martin Luther King Jr. Middle School
Dorchester, 1937

The drawing illustrated two views of the lobby, showing the walls, doors, steps, and curved plaster ceiling. Next to that was a section sliced through the lobby, the balcony above it, and the exterior wall.

Drawing courtesy of Boston Public Schools, Campbell Center.

CHAPTER VI
After the War

I N 1945, WORLD WAR II ENDED AND OUR SOLDIERS BEGAN TO return from Europe and the Far East. By 1950, the men had gone back to work, the women had left their war-time jobs, families were begun, and the baby boom was well underway. In the 1950s more than four million children were born each year and, of course, schools would be needed for these children.[1] Life was back to "normal." But what was normal? After nearly twenty years of depression and war, it was difficult to remember life without worries, disappointments, and problems. The 1950s formed a period of recovery both economically and socially, and formed the concept of the ideal American family. This picture perfect family was to include a father, a mother, two or three children, and a dog living in a house surrounded by green grass and similar neighbors. This ideal family went to church on Sunday, had periodic visits from grandparents, watched themselves on television, were white, protestant, middle class, and lived in the suburbs. There was mild tolerance for deviations from the idealized "normal." Jews, African-Americans, Catholics, single and divorced adults, and nonconformists were outside the ideal picture but were definitely part of everyone's reality. Though extremists supported Senator Joseph McCarthy's subcommittee's investigations of suspected communist sympathizers, in general, people occupied themselves with rebuilding their lives, homes, cities, suburbs, and schools in this period of prosperity.

There were significant shifts in population during the 1950s and Boston was affected by these movements. The city's population peaked at 801,444 in 1950 making it the tenth most populous city in the United States. In only ten years, Boston's population dropped to 697,197 and continued to decline through the 1960s to only 641,071 in 1970.[2] Families moved out of crowded cities and away from the polyglot urban bustle. They went to the suburbs in search of house and lawn that were part of the ideal American family. It meant that middle-class families moved from the Boston neighborhoods to the surrounding towns such as Lexington, Belmont, Needham, and Peabody along Route 128 where corporations were expanding. Unlike earlier decades, there were not large waves of foreign immigrants entering Boston, and other cities, to fill the gap. Due to the enactment of quota legislation in the 1920s, there were fewer immigrants and the proportion of the white, foreign-born population had dropped from 13.4% in 1900 to only 6.7% in 1950.[3] The Boston neighborhood of Charlestown shrunk from 25,000 population in 1950 to 19,000 in 1960. Similarly, the 81,000 people residing in Roxbury in 1960 represented a 25% decrease from 1950.[4]

The new immigrants coming to Boston in the 1950s were not foreign born. They were black Americans migrating from the agrarian South to the industrialized North, from rural to urban areas. In 1954, the United States Supreme Court's decision in Brown v. Topeka Board of Education struck down the "separate but equal" concept for schools. This case demonstrated the predicament for black Americans in the South and their hopes for more opportunities in the North. This migration continued through the 1950s and 1960s. The Boston legend is that the Protestants left Boston to escape from the Irish and the Irish left to escape from the African-Americans.[5] In truth, the prosperity of these decades led middle-class Boston residents to the neighboring towns with new houses, new schools, and new jobs. From 1950 to 1970, 31% of the white population left Boston. It was the substantial decrease in population, as well as the new black migration, that shifted the city's reduced population from 3% to 16% African-American.[6] With these new residents in Boston, there were new challenges for the city government, businesses, and schools to provide opportunities for the adults and their children.

The relative calm of the 1950s culminated in turbulence during the next decade. Ten years of life in the suburbs had not soothed the nerves of middle-class youth who joined the disenfranchised to protest most every subject imaginable. There were protests by blacks, students, youths, hippies, and women against the Vietnam War and for civil rights. The federal government took a stand with the passage of the 1964 Civil Rights Act and the 1965 Voting Rights Act, which would affect both schools and offices. However, even before this, the National Association for the Advancement of Colored People (NAACP) had asked the Massachusetts Commission Against Discrimination (MCAD) to investigate the Boston schools, but MCAD found that race was not a determining factor in assignment or quality.[7] In 1966, the privately funded Operation Exodus transported black children to predominately white public schools in Boston, and METCO sent black children to suburban schools. The struggle continued between the Boston School

Committee and the State Board of Education for implementation of the 1965 Racial Imbalance Act. Meanwhile, the Boston Banks' Urban Renewal Group (BBURG) was formed in 1968 to provide mortgages to low-income black families and the result was that Mattapan became 90% black in three years.[8] People were speaking out as never before and feelings that were once private became the subject of public debate and protest.

The restless spirit of this postwar period was ready to move out to the suburbs, rebuild the cities, and embrace modern architecture. What had started in the 1930s (and was stopped by the war) was picked up again with renewed vigor. The Mystic River Bridge of 1950 connected the northern towns to Boston, while the completion of the Southeast Expressway in 1959 opened the South Shore to commuters. Americans were ready to praise the new and condemn the old. Even in conservative Boston, the 1949 design by Cram & Ferguson for the John Hancock Building was contemporary. By 1953, Mayor Hynes announced that the old West End was to be demolished for new, modern, high- rise apartment buildings. And only a year later, the new, low-income Columbia Point housing project was constructed.[9] What was begun in the 1950s would blossom in the next decade with the establishment of the Boston Redevelopment Authority in 1960.

The New Boston began with major programs for downtown and neighborhood renewal created by the director of the Boston Redevelopment Authority (BRA), Edward Logue. The BRA offices were set up in the City Hall Annex and on the second floor of Quincy Market. Scale models of entire neighborhoods were built, satellite offices established, and large plans were drawn. The emphasis continued to be on the New Boston and definitely not on the old. In 1961, the Callahan Tunnel was opened providing the second tunnel to East Boston, the North Shore and the airport. A major commitment to the new was made with the commencement of Government Center construction and, consequently, the demolition of the old Scollay Square area. Modern architecture and major urban renewal were celebrated again in 1965 with the opening of the Prudential Center and continued on with nearly thirty more downtown office buildings and stores in the next decade.[10] More demolition and renewal were planned by the BRA in the South End, but this time the displaced poor protested, pitched tents, and insisted that their need for low-income housing be acknowledged. By 1969, the symbol for the New Boston was completed; the new city hall formed in "new brutalism" concrete, the most current fashion of architecture, was anchored on the large red brick plaza.

The most significant far reaching event for school buildings during this period was the study, *Boston Schools—1962: A Report on the Schools of Boston* issued in May 1962. As noted in the text "this study was undertaken under contract between the Boston Redevelopment Authority and Harvard University, and with the cooperation of the Mayor, the School Committee, and the School Buildings Commission of the City of Boston."[11]

> *Now as Boston embarks on its Urban Renewal Program, it is significant that early in the development of this major and unique attempt to revitalize the City, the Redevelopment Authority should look to the schools.*[12]

This report on the current status of the schools and future recommendations would be the major guiding document for school buildings during the next twenty years, throughout the 1960s and 1970s. It established the attitudes that dominated this period. Based upon these attitudes, it formulated the actions that were to be taken. As with most studies, not all of its proposals were implemented and its time schedule lagged, but surprisingly much of this study was followed. Five major themes included advocacy of new ideas; abandonment of old schools; construction of new schools; community use; and the citywide campus high school.

The emphasis upon new ideas in this report was typical for planners and architects in the 1960s. People were not interested in preserving or exemplifying the past; traditional teaching methods and old buildings had little merit for this generation. The new was in and the old was out. The Boston Redevelopment Authority's urban renewal goal was to create the New Boston, and this same emphasis upon the new was applied to the schools. The standard class size of 30 students was no longer acceptable. Educators were advocating classes of varying size from 15 to 150. This made the standardized classroom obsolete and movable walls that could create various sized spaces were recommended.[13] To meet changing enrollments across the city, "demountable" classrooms that could be moved from site to site were advocated. Traditional architecture was to be replaced with new materials and construction methods. Steel or concrete structural frames, prestressed concrete beams, large stretches of glass in steel frames, metal curtain walls, and painted or glazed concrete blocks were some of the new materials and methods.

Contemporary school design is quite incompatible in most cases with older schools; therefore, no additions, except where other alternatives do not exist, should be directly attached to existing structures.[14]

The recommended abandonment of older schools reflected the advocacy for the new and the reality of the shrinking population in Boston. As early as 1953, a city study had recommended the abandonment of 63 schools in the next seven years; though this was not fully implemented, by 1960 at least 32 of these schools were closed. The 1962 building evaluation included five factors:[15]
1. Educational suitability
2. Age and type of structure
3. Degree of deterioration
4. Location in relation of population patterns
5. Fire safety

Many of the older schools had wood-frame construction for floors and roofs, though the walls were masonry. This was considered a fire hazard, particularly since it was not customary, or required, to have fire sprinklers throughout schools. More than eighty-one schools were slated for closure dating from 1840 through 1930. All of the fifty-three schools constructed before 1900 were recommended for abandonment. Most of this was eventually accomplished, and by the 1990s, when historic buildings were again fashionable, there were only three remaining: Fuller Elementary School 1892 in Jamaica Plain, Taft Middle School 1895 in Brighton, and Clap Elementary School 1896 in Dorchester.

The construction of new schools in the Boston neighborhoods was the focal point of this educational vision. By definition, new schools were considered better than old schools. Given the condition of many urban schools—due to twenty years of depression and war and another ten years of declining population and revenues—there was certainly cause for alarm. However, some Boston schools had been renovated and additions had been constructed in the 1950s. Between 1957 and 1963, ten new elementary schools were opened and two more by the fall of 1969. The ambitious study recommended seven new buildings and ten additions for junior high schools; and fifty-five new schools plus twelve additions for elementary education. All of this was to be accomplished by 1975. The authors of the 1962 report were responding to middle-class American values and were trying valiantly to stop the migration out of Boston.

> *The city schools—and this is the case with Boston—often lagged behind the suburbs. And it would be difficult to discount or deny the pull these handsome schools had for the people who took their children off the cramped, city streets and placed them down in the bright, airy suburbs.*[16]

The community use of the proposed new schools was of paramount importance for the urban renewal envisioned by the Boston Redevelopment Authority. They proposed that the school buildings be used by other groups and combined with other civic functions such as branch libraries, teenage and adult recreation centers, welfare and public health agencies, adult education centers, senior citizens activities, and neighborhood meetings.

> *"Well designed schools on adequate sites, which are centers of community activity, may go far in arresting blight and improving neighborhoods where residents must establish new confidence in their community.*[17]

The planners were hoping that schools could become focal points for city neighborhoods and symbols for the future. With an emphasis upon families, children, youth, learning, and wholesome activities they hoped to answer the lure of the suburbs for middle-class America. Also, they were trying to address the new challenges of riots and protests, civil disobedience, racial strife, and the increased percentage of students from poor families. Creating a sense of community was their goal and this would influence school design in the subsequent decades.

It was this 1962 Report formulated by Harvard University and the Boston Redevelopment Authority that strongly recommended the large campus high school. These educators were advocating a college scale institution on the high school level. It was their contention that by bringing a large number of students together, organized into smaller academic houses, it would be more feasible and affordable to have special facilities such as swimming pools, gymnasia, TV studios, technology, and shops. Though large, well-equipped high schools had certainly been built in other parts of the country, they considered their idea unique.

> A *high school for so large a number of students as 5,500 is a unique proposition. In fact, 5,500 is so large a number that this school ceases to be a conventional high school at all and should be treated as something new on the educational horizon.*[18]

There were already a number of central high schools in Boston, so that this proposed new high school, though much larger, fell within this group and continued this potential of cutting through neighborhood rivalries, economic levels, and racial barriers.

Urban design was a major intellectual concern in the 1960s combining the professional disciplines of architecture and city planning. The Harvard University Graduate School of Design was a leader in this field under the direction of José Louis Sert. The interest in designing cities, and the confidence that professionals could do just that, had its roots in the earlier modern architecture of Walter Gropius, Mies Van der Rohe, and Le Corbusier, in the 1920s and 1930s. As they and their followers came of age and spread out to the universities, professional organizations, and cities, the concepts of urban design developed. There were no small plans. With bold strokes, the urban designers ripped down the old; built up the new; rearranged and molded; created parks and plazas; enhanced light, air and vistas; and zoned areas for commerce, industry, housing, and education. It was design on the grand scale similar to those bold plans that had created Paris, Rome, Washington D.C., and Boston's Back Bay. The Boston Redevelopment

Authority, established in 1960, was born from these grand, noble, altruistic (and perhaps arrogant) goals. Their concepts for the Boston Public Schools were part of their urban design renewal for the New Boston.

Modern school planning was a national movement and affected urban and suburban schools from California to Massachusetts after World War II. Architects used modern architectural forms and materials in their practices and applied these to their school projects. Educators, planners, and architects led the way and were supported by parents, teachers, and administrators. There were three important beliefs for modern school planning:

1. The school environment should be similar to the domestic environment in scale and atmosphere.
2. The educational program should include training in science, technology, handicrafts, and athletics.
3. The schools should be cultural centers for the communities or neighborhoods.[19]

Some of these ideas had certainly existed in the American educational philosophy before World War II, but now the ideas were codified and voices more uniform. The architectural forms and physical plans of the school buildings were the most radical departure from previous decades. Gone was the traditional imposing dignified red brick edifice with a double loaded corridor. In its place, architects began to experiment with various plan types such as the finger plan, cluster-type plan, loft, core-type plan, and campus plan.

Educational research was supported by foundations and organizations such as the Education Facilities Laboratories (EFL) funded by the Ford Foundation. The EFL was known to most architects practicing in the 1960s, and their findings were usually respected and followed by the profession. EFL encouraged innovations in school planning and architecture through conferences and publications. Chicago architect C. William Brubaker in his 1998 book, *Planning and Designing Schools* reminisced over the "research and extension" and four principles promoted by the EFL: the use of movable walls to provide flexibility for various sized teaching groups; the use of system building components to bring the efficiency of the factory to building construction; the use of the new media, television, to connect the classroom to the world; and new organizational methods to include team teaching, new curricula, and community involvement.[20] All of these principles, and particularly the concept of the open plan, were to have profound effects upon school design in the coming decades. The 1960s was a period of personal freedom, civil disobedience, and social innovation. Educational innovation was part of this mentality as educators sought new methods to prepare young people for the post World War II world.

The effects upon Boston schools were more muted than innovative educators might have wanted in the 1960s. This was perhaps due to natural conservatism, a lack of funding, a decreasing student population, and an abundance of existing schools, but change did definitely occur. Most of the new schools had simple, straight-forward plans with the double loaded corridors similar to traditional schools. Aside from that, things were quite different. There were no grand entries, the buildings were low to the ground, the small scale was for children, bearing walls had been changed to concrete frames, and wood windows had become steel. Most important was the transformation in size. The pre World War II Boston elementary schools averaged about 35,000 square feet and now the schools were about 52,000 square feet.[21] This increased size was partly due to the special facilities that were considered essential for a well-equipped school. These could include a lunchroom, auditorium, gymnasium, nurse's suite, library, and other administrative rooms. However, the ideas of the 1960s advocated substantial changes in school design and set the stage for radical innovation in the next decade for Boston.

FOOTNOTES

1. Brubaker, C. William, *Planning and Designing Schools* (New York, McGraw-Hill, 1998) p. 42.

2. "12 Moments That Mattered 1872–1997," *The Boston Globe Magazine*, March 2, 1997, pp. 33, 34, 37.

3. *Encyclopaedia Britannica* (Chicago, Encyclopaedia Britannica, Inc., William Benton, Publishers, 1962) Volume 22, p. 817.

4. *Boston Schools—1962: A Report on the Schools of Boston*, This study was undertaken under a contract between the Boston Redevelopment Authority and Harvard University and with the cooperation of the Mayor, the School Committee, and the School Buildings Commission of the City of Boston. May 1962. p. II-3, p. II-69.

5. Formisano, Ronald P., *Boston Against Busing* (Chapel Hill, The University of North Carolina Press, 1991) p. 13.

6. Ibid, p. 13.

7. Formisano, op. cit., p. 28.

8. Formisano, op. cit., pp. 13, 37–38.

9. *The Boston Globe Magazine*, op. cit.

10. Ibid.

11. *Boston Schools—1962*, op. cit., p. 3.

12. Ibid, p. x.

13. Ibid, p. I-16.

14. Ibid, p. I-53.

15. Ibid, p. xiii.

16. Ibid, p. I-ii.

17. Ibid, p. xi.

18. Ibid, p. I-39.

19. *Encyclopedia Britannica*, op. cit., Volume 7, p. 992.

20. Brubaker, C. William, *Planning and Designing Schools* (McGraw-Hill, New York, 1998) pp. 16, 20.

21. Wallace, Floyd, Associates, Inc., *Boston Public School Facilities Overview,* January 14, 1994, Phase 1: Volume 2, Inventory and Condition Report, p. 19.

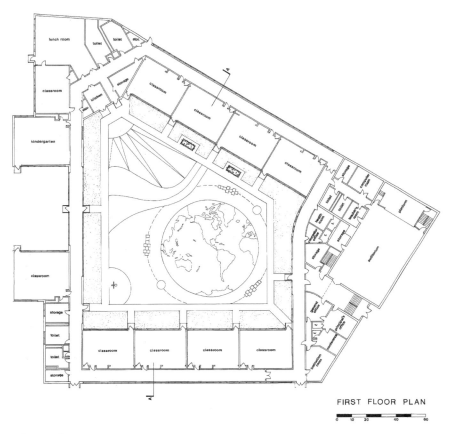

FIRST FLOOR PLAN

0 10 20   40   60

Floor Plan
Patrick O'Hearn Elementary School
Dorchester, 1957

This small elementary school included ten classrooms and one kindergarten room surrounding a play courtyard. It was well planned with a lunchroom, auditorium, administrative offices, and health suite. The low one-story building was scaled for children as advocated in the 1950s. The unique plan had the building surrounding the perimeter of the site thereby enclosing the center to create a controlled environment for activities and views. The school was named after Dorchester resident, Patrick O'Hearn, former president of the Hibernia Savings Bank, who served as Boston's building commissioner from 1914 to 1917. *Drawing courtesy of Cole and Goyette, Architects and Planners Inc.*

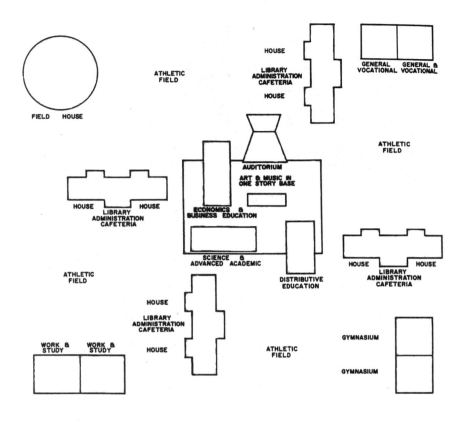

KEY TO PROPOSED CAMPUS HIGH SCHOOL

0   100   200   300   400
SCALE   IN   FEET

Boston Schools—1962:
A Report on the Schools of Boston

The educators from Harvard University who wrote this report in the 1960s recommended this large urban campus high school plan for Boston. In 1978 their vision became reality with the construction of the Madison Park High School campus plan with 888,312 square feet of floor space. *Illustration courtesy of Boston Public Schools.*

CHAPTER VII
Suburban Spread

TURMOIL AND RENEWAL CONTINUED IN THE 1970S. FAMILY roots had been cut and the American population continued to shift from country to city, from city to suburb, from South to North and East to West. Traditional restraints were loosened and people acted out fantasies and fears as never before. "Let it all hangout" was the expression of the day and people did just that talking endlessly about their personal feelings, loves, hates, and opinions. Of course, this affected personal and family relations, but it also affected the relationships among groups in neighborhoods, politics, and institutions such as schools. This open discussion was at times beneficial and productive. However, it could become confrontational and aggressive. On the national level, President Johnson's emphasis upon civil rights for women and minorities continued, Nixon left office due to the Watergate scandal, Ford filled the incompleted term, and then Carter ended the decade with Americans held hostage at our embassy in Iran. On the local level in Boston, similar tumultuous movements catapulted us through the 1970s with racial tensions and busing, economic ups and downs, population shifts and declines, and construction, demolition, and renewal. Though on the national level leaders had come and gone, in Boston one person presided over this decade: Kevin White, mayor from 1968 to 1984.

Boston's population continued to decline at a rapid rate. In the 1970s the population dropped another 14% from 641,071 to 562,994 by 1980. The continuing migration of African-Americans into Boston was not sufficient to avoid the total urban population from declining significantly. With this decline in the general population, there was also a reduction in the number of children attending Boston public schools. As the prosperous middle class moved out to new houses and new schools in the surrounding suburbs, the poor were left behind. By 1979, it was reported that 30% of Boston residents lived in poverty.[1] Children fared worst with 61% of the students at or below the federal poverty level.[2] The trend was for the poor to live in the city and the middle class to live in the suburbs. With this shift in wealth came a shift in political and social influence. Though suburbanites did not vote in Boston, they were the business and cultural leaders in Boston and the commuters who worked in the offices. They brought with them each day a thirst for the New Boston of the central core. Though the population in the neighborhoods declined producing empty lots and abandoned buildings, the central district remained firm producing infilled lots and new buildings.

Most of the changes seen by visitors and commuters were in central Boston. The urban renewal started in the 1960s by the Boston Redevelopment Authority continued through the 1970s. The construction of Government Center proceeded with the 1970 State Health Education and Welfare Building by architect Paul Rudolph with a grey rough bush-hammered concrete exterior. Concrete was again selected over red brick for the 1970 Government Center Garage by architects Kallmann and McKinnell with Samuel Glaser. The fashionable concrete persisted in the 1971 Harbor Towers apartments near the modern concrete Aquarium and through the decade to the 1979 John F. Kennedy Library by I.M. Pei in South Boston. This lust for the new was tempered by a reawakened appreciation for the buildings that made Boston unique. For example, when the wholesale food market left Quincy Market for larger quarters, the old building was not torn down but transformed into the Faneuil Hall Market Place by architect Benjamin Thompson. The concept of the suburban shopping mall was transformed into the urban mall at Faneuil Hall. By 1974, the old Charlestown Navy Yard was being transformed into a multi use residential and retail development.[3] This combination of new and old in downtown Boston would spread out eventually to the neighborhoods and would greatly affect the construction and preservation of Boston schools.

The racial tensions of the 1960s peaked in the 1970s. The conflict focused on the schools, but spilled out into the neighborhoods affecting housing, offices, and most aspects of city life. Central Boston remained neutral territory where all could meet, but neighborhoods disintegrated and tempers flared. The 1965 Massachusetts Racial Imbalance Act continued to be enforced, and by 1971, the State Board of Education ordered an immediate freeze on $200 million worth of new construction in Boston and withdrew $14 million in state aid. Though this was later overturned in court, the battle went on towards desegregation. By October 1973, the Massachusetts Supreme Judicial Court ordered the Boston School Committee to begin implementing the state desegregation plan.[4] Compliance was insufficient and, therefore, a year later the matter was in federal court.

On June 21, 1974, U.S. District Judge W. Arthur Garrity, Jr. ruled that Boston school committees over the years had deliberately maintained racial segregation in the city's schools, thereby violating the constitutional rights of black students to the best available education.[5]

Judge Garrity's remedy was busing, and he oversaw the implementation of this plan for the next eleven years. It was not a popular plan. Though many schools integrated quietly, there was strife in some of the neighborhood schools, such as South Boston and Hyde Park High Schools. Police were in the schools to maintain order, and the learning environment was difficult.

The racial conflicts in the neighborhoods and schools were part of the long history of immigration in the United States. Boston's reception to new immigrants over the last 200 years was no different than other cities—be it New York, Chicago, Dallas, or San Francisco. Life could be difficult for immigrants. There were language and cultural barriers, poverty, often menial work, inadequate housing, broken families, rebellious children, and social humiliations. The first immigrants to the Massachusetts Bay Colony displaced the Native Americans in the 1600s; the rebellious colonialists ejected the British in the 1700s; the Irish immigrants arrived and many of the earlier settlers moved on to the surrounding towns in the early 1800s; Italians, Jews, and Eastern European immigrants arrived in the late 1800s moving through Boston. By 1900, fifty percent of the city was of foreign stock. However, the 1924 immigration legislation stopped this flow. For the next twenty-five years there were no large waves of new immigrants; there were movements in and around Boston as a livable balance was established. Finally, this balance was disrupted in the 1950s as waves of people moved out of the city, and in the 1960s and 1970s as the new immigrants, African-Americans, moved into Boston. "Diane Ravitch, the historian of New York City's 'school wars' from 1805 to 1973, described a succession of struggles between different religious, cultural, and racial groups, coinciding roughly with each new wave of immigration into the city."[6] Such struggles were similar in many cities.

As usual, Americans, and many Bostonians, looked to the public schools to right the wrongs of society. The nineteenth-century belief that the path to success was through education continued to be a guiding principle in the twentieth century. In fact, the universal acceptance of this belief in education fueled the demands of black Americans for equal schools. The concept of public education for all children, which did not exist in early twentieth-century Europe and was revolutionary in America, was now totally expected by all citizens. Through this century, American and Boston schools had been expected to educate children as well as provide discipline, instill moral values, produce skilled workers, promote healthful habits, and prepare immigrant children to meld into American society. Now the federal government and the Commonwealth of Massachusetts had determined that the public schools were to support the civil rights of women and minorities. In 1972, the Boston Latin School, the oldest public school in this country, admitted female students.[7] This was one of many educational institutions to become coeducational in the 1970s. Along with this, busing and other measures began to integrate both black and white children in schools. It was determined that separate schools could not be equal, that an important part of education was for young people to learn how to live and work with people different from themselves.

As the Boston population continued to decline, more schools were closed and new ones were built. Sixty-two older schools were demolished or sold and used for other purposes such as housing or offices.[8] With an abundance of schools, the city kept the buildings that met the five evaluation factors that had been established by the study *Boston Schools—1962: A Report On the Schools of Boston* prepared by the Boston Redevelopment Authority (BRA) and Harvard University. The five factors of educational suitability; age and type of structure; degree of deterioration; location; and fire safety were, of course, important, but other factors such as political clout and neighborhood pressures saved many of these historic schools. These closures were offset by the construction of twenty-three new schools scattered throughout the various Boston neighborhoods. They included seventeen elementary schools, one middle school, and five high schools. While the populous stewed over busing, Mayor Kevin White pushed on with an ambitious building program that produced more than two new schools per year. The pre World War II schools that were not demolished received few renovations during this decade. The emphasis at the state and city levels was upon the new and, therefore, available money was spent upon new buildings.

These new schools embodied the new ideas for education, architecture, and planning and have had a lasting effect on the Boston public schools.

These new schools were very different from the traditional Boston schools. Sixteen of the seventeen elementary schools constructed between 1967 and 1977 had some form of open plan, though they all included a few closed classrooms.[9] Gone were the traditional double-loaded corridors lined with classrooms composed of walls, doors, and windows. All of the classroom standards that had been developed by the Boston Schoolhouse Department over the past seventy years had been tossed out by educators and, consequently, by their architects. Educators were advocating team teaching, individualized learning programs for students, and freedom of movement and thought. Children located in defined rooms and seated in straight rows were considered too restricted. Self expression was in, conformity was out. These notions were applied by educators to new schools from the West Coast to the East Coast. Many of these new schools were in towns and suburbs populated by the middle class. This suburban model spread into the Boston neighborhoods of both the middle class and the poor. The freedom and self expression encouraged in the open classroom sometimes was tainted by the aggression of the urban streets. Though some teachers resisted, it generally was a time to experiment with new teaching methods that would encourage students towards creative thinking.

The school buildings constructed in the 1970s were much larger than in previous decades. There were more square feet of floor space per pupil than ever before. This was due to the size of the classrooms plus other amenities such as cafeterias, libraries, gymnasia, swimming pools, and auditoria. Along with this came increased space for community use of schools including adult education and training, community and neighborhood associations, and sports and club groups. Though "a numerical majority of Boston's active school buildings were built before World War II, including two from the 1890s,"[10] the schools from this decade dominated in area. In these ten years, 40% of the system's 10 million square feet was constructed. For example, only six of the city's sixteen high schools were constructed in the 1970s, yet they dominated with 47% of the total square feet devoted to high school education. About the same number of high school students occupied

255,000 square feet in 1970 that had previously been schooled in only 175,000 square feet. The statistics for the elementary schools were even more telling.

> *The seventeen elementary schools (22% of total number) in this cate-*
> *gory [built during 1970s] comprise almost 50% of the total area of ele-*
> *mentary schools. Their average size of 125,000 square feet is more than*
> *three times the average size of schools constructed prior to this time.*[11]

Bigger was definitely considered better as the politicians and educators tried to equalize educational opportunities, renew decaying neighborhoods, and revitalize the school system.

In plan and space, these schools varied significantly from previous decades. The floor plans were a radical departure from the straight double-loaded corridor lined with classrooms. While the open plan and clustered classrooms expressed new teaching methods, the spatial organization and circulation patterns went far beyond this. The simplicity of early modern architecture with clean lines, open space, and self-evident geometry developed into complexity. The architect's goal was to create a progression of interesting and varied spaces that would be experienced by students and teachers. In rebellion to the mandates of classical architecture, these plans were not symmetrical. Entrances were not to be located in the center of a facade, and the two ends were to look different. The rebellion that had started in the 1930s, grew in the professional academies of the 1960s, and blossomed in the schoolyards in the 1970s. By this decade, the right-angle was out of fashion and the 45° angle was in. Varied volumes and spaces were to define activities. The goal was to modulate and shape space; to provide interesting spatial experiences as one walked through or used a space. With this in mind, architects raised and lowered ceiling heights. Walls were angled in plan and elevation. Floors were at varying levels connected by ramps and stairs. The new architecture complemented and expressed contemporary concepts for education.

The construction materials for the new schools deviated from the traditional Boston buildings. Though some of the new schools had brick exteriors, such as the 1971 Harvard-Kent School in Charlestown, in general they were concrete. The old red brick schoolhouse had been supplanted by the new grey concrete school facility. These grey buildings were covered with textured concrete blocks or precast concrete panels; poured concrete was used for columns, floors, and some walls. The brick bearing walls of the old schools were replaced with concrete block bearing walls. However, the post and beam steel construction that became prevalent in the 1960s schools continued and was varied with reinforced concrete posts and beams. These structural systems could provide the large flexible spaces needed for the open classrooms advocated by educators. Over the years, there had also been significant engineering advances in systems for heating, ventilating, and air conditioning. Though at times complex and experimental, these systems were installed in the new schools. The old, wood, double-hung windows gave way to new steel-frame hopper vent windows. The strength of the steel allowed the frames to be thin providing a profile favored by architects. It was a time to embrace the new, and this included the materials that were being manufactured and developed by industrial America.

The sites were considerably larger for these sizable new schools. The traditional elementary schools generally had small play yards and often the high schools had no athletic fields. These standards were no longer acceptable in the 1970s. For example, nationwide the ideal size for a high school site increased from about two city blocks in 1900 to forty acres after World War II to as much as fifty acres in 1970.[12] Of course, there was considerably less land in the East and, therefore, these standards were scaled back around Boston. However, the city did strive towards increased outdoor space and succeeded at schools such as the Lee Elementary School and Charlestown High School that are adjacent to large play fields. When land was not available, roof- top play areas were developed as at the central city 1976 Quincy School. Generally, these schools were restricted to one or two stories and spread out over the land. It was how these schools met the land that was new and unusual. The ground floor flowed over the land molding itself to the contours of the natural terrain. With ramps and steps, the floor level changed bringing interest to the corridors, spaces, and views to the exterior. Nature was to be respected and preserved with the building molding itself around natural features such as trees, rocky outcroppings, knolls, and valleys. In truth, many of the sites designated for school construction were difficult remainders, unwanted by others, filled with ledge and rocky hills that would need to be removed to create the efficient flat site. Therefore, the architects tried to make a design feature of the site presented and melded architecture and nature on the rolling landscape.

Boston was in the forefront of school construction in the 1970s. Throughout the country, the children born during the baby boom of the early 1950s had completed their schooling and enrollment was dropping. Many school districts soon had too much space and were confronted with the choices of selling buildings; leasing buildings; keeping buildings for use by new programs; or keeping buildings mothballed for future use.[13] Building new schools or even making major improvements to existing schools were not popular expenditures in these communities. Boston confronted declining student enrollment very differently and boldly. The city closed old schools and built new ones. Forced by the courts to provide equal educational opportunity and determined to keep Boston a vital urban center, the leaders decided to build. The Commonwealth of Massachusetts helped to finance this construction, but it was the mayor and his advisors who decided to follow the concepts laid out in the 1962 Boston Schools Report. It was this construction boom that gave the city and its architects the opportunity to excel while many educational systems languished due to enrollment declines and economic dips. In ten years, Boston built more than four million square feet of space.[14]

Boston was a major center for contemporary architectural training and practice. As leaders in their field, these Boston architects and their national colleagues applied their skills to the proposed schools. Striving for the innovative and unique, the schools varied greatly in plan, volume, and space. However, there were some standards which were formulated in the systems specifications that described the various materials and construction procedures that were to be followed in these buildings. The 1972 Holland Elementary School was designed by architect Benjamin Thompson, who would become nationally known for the Faneuil Hall Market Place, the Design Research building in Cambridge, and numerous other projects far beyond Dorchester. Architects who generally designed schools in towns and suburbs turned their eyes towards Boston as did Earl Flansburgh with the 1971

Harvard-Kent School in Charlestown. The bastion of modern design, The Architects Collaborative (TAC) applied its skills to the 1976 Josiah Quincy Elementary School in Boston. For each project, the architects enthusiastically embraced and promoted the concepts and forms of modern architecture. Perhaps in their quest to be unique leaders among their peers, some embraced the new without sufficient consideration of past or future paths.

The bureaucratic organizations for the construction of Boston schools had been altered dramatically since 1962. Of course, the elected School Committee was still in place, but the Schoolhouse Department and the Department of School Buildings that had guided school planning and construction from the turn of the century were gone. By 1970, the new Public Facilities Department was firmly established to guide all new public construction including schools. On the other hand, the School Department of Planning and Engineering was in charge of repairs and alterations. The responsibility for planning schools was no longer separated from other buildings and was no longer the sole prerogative of the Boston Public School department. There was greater reliance upon outside experts to do studies and provide policy recommendations on education. Also, many of the building and space standards were being set by the state Department of Education since it was providing more financial support. There were no precise lists of spatial standards and sheets of detailed drawings as done by the Schoolhouse Department for architects to study and follow. From the architectural results, there appears to have been greater freedom for interpretation of educational needs. The establishment of the Public Facilities Department exemplified the link between urban renewal and new schools in the neighborhoods.

Along with the frenzy for the new, awareness of the old persisted. The renovation of the Quincy Market buildings into an urban mall and the transformation of the Charlestown Navy Yard into housing and offices were two examples of saving old buildings. Along with this, many historic schools had been made into housing in Boston and the suburbs. Gradually people realized that Boston history might be good economics. American tourists liked this city because it looked different from their home towns; European tourists liked Boston because it looked similar to their cities left behind. Downtown Boston was a lively mixture of the very new and the old. For the schools, the conversion of the 1882 Boston Art Club into a public high school in 1970 was a hint of what the 1980s would bring. This relatively small 36,400 square foot building located on fashionable Newbury Street was certainly different from the new high schools of 255,000 square feet. Not only was the building smaller, but the number of students was reduced to fit this cozy former clubhouse. Boston was a national leader in 1970s contemporary architecture and would continue to apply this Yankee ingenuity in the coming decades.

FOOTNOTES

1. Wallace, Floyd, Associates, Inc., *Boston Public School Facilities Overview,* January 14, 1994, Phase 1: Volume 2, Inventory and Condition Report, p. 3.

2. Formisano, Ronald P., *Boston Against Busing* (Chapel Hill, The University of North Carolina Press, 1991) p. 25.

3. "12 Moments that Mattered 1872–1997," *The Boston Globe Magazine*, March 2, 1997, p. 39.

4. Lukas, J. Anthony, *Common Ground*, (New York, Alfred A. Knopf, 1985), pp. 218, 219.

5. Mulvoy Jr., Thomas F., "Buses and Bitterness," *The Boston Globe Magazine*, March 1997, p. 43.

6. Formisano, op. cit., p. 220.

7. *The Boston Globe Magazine*, op. cit., p. 37.

8. List of Closed Boston Public Schools, Revised 1991, Boston Public Schools Department.

9. Wallace, Floyd, Associates Inc., op. cit., p. 22.

10. Ibid, p. 22.

11. Ibid, p. 22.

12. Brubaker, William C., *Planning and Designing Schools* (New York, McGraw- Hill, 1998) p. 165.

13. Ibid, p. 22.

14. Wallace, Floyd, Associates, Inc., op. cit., p. 11.

Older schools tend to have simple geometric plans with few "nooks & crannies" in circulation space. Most student-oriented doors open directly onto corridors, as shown in this example.

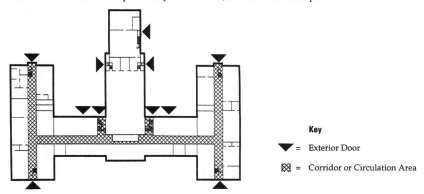

Key

▼ = Exterior Door

▨ = Corridor or Circulation Area

Edison Middle School, built in 1932

In contrast, the 1970's schools often have complex circulation patterns and too many doors. For instance, the street level of the Hennigan School has 21 sets of exterior doors. Many doors do not open onto the main circulation corridor. Circulation is complex on the first and upper floors.

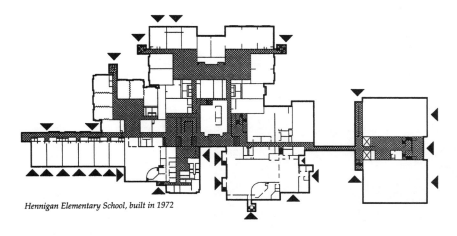

Hennigan Elementary School, built in 1972

Inventory and Condition Analysis
Boston Public School Facilities Overview
Boston, 1993

This page was from the report prepared by Wallace, Floyd, Associates, Inc. for the Boston Public Facilities Department. It compared and contrasted the entries and circulation patterns of the Edison Middle School, built in 1932, and the Hennigan Elementary School, built in 1972, revealing the greater complexity of a typical layout of the 1970s. *Illustration courtesy of Boston Public Schools.*

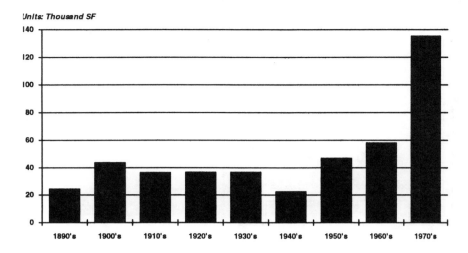

Units: Thousand SF

Average size of elementary schools, by decade built

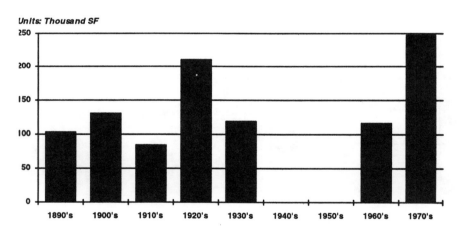

Units: Thousand SF

Average size of middle and high schools, by decade built

Inventory and Condition Analysis
Boston Public School Facilities Overview
Boston, 1993

As illustrated on these charts from the Wallace, Floyd, Associates, Inc. report, the size of both elementary and high schools increased greatly during the 1970s. The schools were larger primarily due to more support spaces and diverse teaching areas. *Illustration courtesy of the Boston Public Schools.*

CHAPTER VIII

Turning the Century— Again

THE TURNING OF THE LAST CENTURY WAS EXCITING AND, AS we plan for the twenty-first century and the new millennium, excitement is in the air again. It is a time to assess where we are and where we want to go. People look at their own lives and their communities, governments, and schools. Of course, there are predictions for the future and, as we know from the past, these predictions usually are not quite right. There are many similarities between the turning of the last century and this century that color our vision for the twenty-first century and how we are preparing our schools to fulfill that vision. Economic volatility, civic stability, population growth, technological advances, and national ideals and realities are among those factors that affected the turning of the last century and will affect the twenty-first century. When we look to the past, we learn how those conditions changed cities and towns, adults and children, and work and education. Now we look towards the future, perhaps with little interest in the past. Yet these same factors continue to affect our lives with new twists and turns as we try to understand what is happening now and what might happen in the future.

Economic volatility continued similar to a hundred years ago. In the fall of 1987, the stock market dropped significantly and people were in shock. The consequences were felt throughout the economy with many people losing their jobs as companies "down- sized," i.e., got smaller. Without extra money people bought less and the general economy slumped further. According to the Federal Reserve Bank of Boston, "The regional economy turned down in 1989 and recession hit hard in 1990, but incomes began to rise again in 1992."[1] Also, education was a dominant factor in determining the rise or fall of incomes. While college educated workers made gains, high school dropouts and even some high school graduates saw declines.[2] With the need for more education to perform mid-level jobs, recent immigrants from 1985 to 1989 earned 32% less than natives.[3] Children in Boston were greatly affected since they often came from households headed by single females or new immigrants with less education. Poverty was found in many urban areas such as Minneapolis where 67% of the students qualified for free or reduced-price lunches.[4] Similar to economic conditions in 1900, one hundred years later there were still many poor people in our city, and it was the Boston public schools that guided and educated their children so that as adults they could rise with the economic tides.

Civic stability had been challenged and tested, but endured through the 1980s and 1990s. The continuing Boston saga of school busing rolled on through these decades, fortunately with less violence and strife, but by 1998, the school enrollment was 75% black or Latinos, 16% white, and 9% Asians.[5] Even in 1996, admission policies favoring African-Americans at Boston Latin School were challenged by prospective white students. Local politics, as usual, were lively, but both Mayor Flynn, who took office in 1984, and Mayor Menino, who followed, continued the renewal of public school buildings. However, this civic stability was not reflected in urban households.

Remarkably, only 13% of all households consist of traditional married couples with children.[6]

Teenagers, often still in high school, became unwed mothers trying to cope with their studies and child while unable to support themselves financially. The sexual freedom of the 1960s had grown into the sexual chaos of the 1990s. Improved birth control that had spawned the sexual revolution was no longer being consistently used; the potentially deadly social disease of AIDS was spreading; and drugs, guns, and gangs were still present. Certainly, these conditions were not new to urban life. One need only read a Dickens novel to know that similar conditions existed in nineteenth-century London. But by the late 1990s attitudes had changed towards welfare benefits for single mothers. The public was no longer willing to pay, time limits were set, and able-bodied recipients were expected to get jobs after two years. All of these social realities affected the Boston public schools. It was still expected that education could both curb and cure these social ills.

Population growth at the end of the twentieth century "has historical parallels in the last great migration, which took place at the turn of the century."[7] It was estimated that about ten million immigrants arrived during the 1980s and, since the native birthrate had declined, immigration accounted for about one-third of the population growth in America. Unlike a hundred years ago, this wave of new arrivals was not from Europe: 83% were from Asia or Latin America, 25% from Mexico, and only 15% from Europe or Canada.[8] This change was due to the repeal of the 1924 National Origins Act that restricted immigration and the 1965 increase in available visas. Also, prosperity in Europe decreased movement to America. Though the gates were opened again, the immigrant's life in Boston could still be difficult.

> *Yet newcomers still arrive, bringing vitality and imagination and change. Half of the city's current residents [in 1997] did not live here a decade ago, and most of the newcomers have come from Latin America and Africa and Asia. What historian (and Dorchester native) Theodore White called 'the ethnic ballet' continues at an accelerated tempo as Boston renews and redefines itself.*[9]

These new arrivals were mostly nonwhite or Hispanic and the Federal Reserve Bank of Boston reported that "the gap in schooling between less-educated immigrants and U.S. natives grew from one to three years between 1978 and 1998."[10] There were fears that these people might have more difficulties assimilating successfully into American life. However, the last great wave of immigrants in the early twentieth century showed that it could take two or three generations to assimilate into economic prosperity. Remarkably, though hard work and some luck was acknowledged to keep immigrants from remaining in poverty, even bankers emphasized education—the schools—to train, motivate, and prepare immigrant children for economic success.[11]

Technological advances in the early 1900s dominated employment opportunities just as they did in the late 1900s. Before this, it was the expanding industrialization that needed literate and skilled workers in the factories. One hundred years later it was expanding computerization that needed literate and skilled workers in the offices. To say that computers had freed workers from repetitive and tedious tasks of the factory assembly line might be mistaken when considering the tasks of data entry, but clever computer programs were able to calculate, sort, search, and respond as never before. Though the intrinsic value of computers might be questioned and the intellectual contribution doubted, most people realized that we were midstream and changes would continue probably at a rapid pace in the twenty-first century. For young people searching for employment, particularly at mid- and entry-level jobs, computer literacy was essential, and from 1994 to 1999, there was remarkable growth in the skills of young employees. It was the schools that were again stretching beyond the 3 Rs—reading, writing, and arithmetic—and beyond laboratory science, industrial arts, and home economics to contemporary technology for teaching, learning, and communicating.

Though the quest for the new continued, a renewed interest in old Boston intensified in the 1980s and 1990s. New buildings continued to be constructed, but there was more intense scrutiny and questioning by citizen groups. The demolition of the old Scollay Square for the new Government Center and the demolition of the old West End for the new Charlesgate Apartments were no longer lauded. The modern architecture of the 1970s was out of fashion and historic architecture was valued. This change in attitude had profound effects upon the Boston schools. Under court order to integrate the schools and to equalize opportunity for children of all races, there was a surge of renovation in the 1980s. The Unified Facilities Plan brought renewed life to the older schools of Boston, but even with this, more than thirty schools were closed during this decade. This change in policy towards renewal was startling and perhaps reflected economic realities: It was less expensive to renovate than to build new; the quality of many remaining schools could not be duplicated at a reasonable cost; and there was a sufficient number of existing school buildings. Consequently, no new schools were constructed for eighteen years, 1980 to 1998. It was this surge of renovations that began to uncover, polish, and renew the architectural treasures of the Boston public schools.

Boston was unique in its approach to historic school buildings. While most suburban towns in Massachusetts tore down older schools or mutilated them beyond recognition, Boston renovated and rejuvenated. This decision was perhaps possible due to two factors. First, the Boston schools (remaining after many closures) were a remarkable collection of buildings that had been state-of-the-art when constructed. These buildings were solidly built with fine and durable materials; their spacious and generic designs were adaptable to new teaching methods. Second, the Boston schools were under court order to equalize educational opportunities. This court order was being administrated by a federal judge; it was to proceed in a timely fashion; and it was above local attitudes. The 1960s and 1970s preference for new schools had continued into the 1980s and at the state Department of Education, there was confidence in new construction and suspicion of the old. However, even though the state was funding 90% of the cost, it had little control over this federally approved Boston plan that relied upon renovation of existing historic schools. Therefore, Boston proceeded along its own path, first alone then eventually followed by many, towards the rejuvenation, renovation, and expansion of historic schools for the twenty-first century.

The guidelines issued by the state Department of Education shaped school buildings. Since the state reimbursed cities and towns for school construction, it had developed regulations to insure that the money was being spent prudently. These recommendations covered size and general features of the site; size and quantity of classrooms; size and variety of other amenities; durability of construction; and other matters. These recommendations evolved through time with an emphasis upon new schools in the 1960s and 1970s moving towards renovation and expansion of existing schools in the 1990s. As with most entities in American government, its policies were formed through continuing discussion—with educators, administrators, and architects about school buildings.

> The Commonwealth's School Facilities Assistance Bureau (SFAB), which assists cities and towns in planning and financing schools, generates the dominant standards for Massachusetts facilities.[12]

At times, one might ask if the state led or followed, but in truth, it reflected the will of the people and the current trends in education. Though the guidelines were sketchy and flexible, the requirements to have a cafetorium, library/media center, student computers in every classroom, gymnasium, nurse's suite, special education classrooms, bilingual classrooms, remedial classrooms, and many other facilities molded the buildings. Our concept of what was an adequate school had also been shaped and reshaped by these evolving guidelines that continued to change as we planned for the next century.

Technology brought significant changes to school design. Many of those changes we didn't see directly, but they have impacted our visual environments. For example, if you turned your eyes towards the ceiling of a typical new school of the 1990s, there was a hung acoustical tile ceiling similar to a contemporary office building. Gone were the plaster or concrete ceilings of previous decades. Above that acoustical tile ceiling were an enormous number of ducts, pipes, cables, wires, conduits, sensors, fans, heaters, coolers, sprinklers, detectors, valves, traps, alarms, and controls for the complicated systems that were considered essential for an up-to-date school. Towards the end of the century, it was the computer that dominated our thoughts and challenged our adaptability. If anything, the computer should have forewarned us to design for change. In the 1980s, separate computer classrooms were provided; by the late 1990s the general classrooms were made larger to include a line of computers plugged into the wall; and by the late 2000s these might be replaced with portable computer notebooks. We might remember the accommodations for past technology such as telephone rooms, movable partitions, fixed windows, gravity ducts, and coal bins. Certainly, the past has demonstrated that technology comes and goes, expands and contracts, but through all this, the building endures, providing spaces for children to think, learn, imagine, and dream.

Changing demographics influenced educational programs and buildings. As in most urban areas, Boston had many school-age children in poverty and, significantly, the U.S. Department of Education reported that it cost more to educate poor students.[13] Fortunately, in Massachusetts, the Department of Education had offset some of the additional costs for special programs and classes and, consequently, for equipment, rooms, and buildings. For the first time in forty years, the population of Boston increased from 562,994 in 1980 to 574,283 in 1990. Of course, it was still far from its peak of 801,444 in 1950.[14] Though the total population had increased slightly, there was still a 20% drop in school-age children from 1980 to 1990. While the percentage of both white and black children dropped, immigrant children rose. This contributed to the increase of nearly 70% Asian and 30% Hispanic among school-age children in Boston. Added to this were the teenage mothers, female-headed households, reduced welfare, and increased employment to make ends meet. These factors and others led to more after-school programs and care of young children. Of course, for the after-school programs, it meant rearranging and reequipping those perpetually flexible Boston schools. For the care of young children, another approach was taken. Given the scarcity of large kindergarten rooms and the current state regulations, the city decided to build new and constructed three early learning centers for kindergarten and pre-kindergarten children in 1998. Scattered across the city in the path of population flow, these first new buildings in nineteen years responded to an educational issue that was of concern throughout the nation.

The developing policy of including all children in shared classrooms, whether they be physically handicapped, mentally slow, or emotionally troubled, influenced school planning. In 1993, the Boston public schools reported that 73% of the students were assigned to regular programs, 10% to special education, and 15% to bilingual. In the 1980s, the special needs children were placed in small groups to receive personalized attention; therefore, smaller rooms were needed. In the late 1990s, the approach changed. Special needs children were integrated into classes with other children; consequently, larger classrooms were needed. In the 2000s, this approach might change again affecting classroom sizes once more. Making schools, and all buildings, accessible to physically handicapped people, especially those in wheelchairs, had profoundly influenced architectural design. The modulation of space through changes of level was no longer allowed. The dignified stairways of the 1900s became the unlawful barriers of the 1990s. The varied floor levels of the 1970s were considered unacceptable by the 1990s. These and other policies have been implemented, but, as we know, they will continue to be refined and changed over the coming decades.

A major inventory and analysis report on the Boston public schools was completed in 1994 by the Boston Public Facilities Department. This report, *Boston Public School Facilities Overview*, presented many interesting statistics and, also, contemporary attitudes towards school buildings. It was considered to be the first step in the Master Plan for the Boston Public Schools.[15] Four of their conclusions were as follows:

1. Schools were in surprisingly good condition due to renovations of the 1980s and 1990s, but most buildings still needed more work.
2. The school system was not overcrowded, but it did not have much excess space.
3. Though the numerical majority of the schools were constructed before World War II, more than 40% of the square footage was

constructed in the 1970s.

4. About half of the schools were small compared to the current state Department of Education standards.

Though these findings seem rather benign, their implications and consequences will be crucial for the next decades in the twenty-first century. These four conclusions, though particular to Boston, were similar to issues in many communities.

First, the schools were found to be in acceptable conditions, but needed more renovations. The buildings certainly were not crumbling, many treasures had been restored, and upgrading continued. However, as we know, any building, old or new, needs continuous repair, maintenance, fixing, painting, and care. The Burke High School was one example of the constant care needed to maintain the fragile balance. Opened in 1934, the Burke was a large modern high school for girls, continuing on successfully through 1970. However, ten years later, it was a troubled co-educational high school in disrepair, but "by 1990, the Burke was being written up in national magazines as one of the country's outstanding high schools."[16] By 1995 the situation had changed again and the school lost its accreditation. After renovations to the building and a change in administration, the Burke High School was back on track in 1996. Though this might be an unusual example and a well-painted classroom might not raise test scores, the physical condition of municipal buildings that have a replacement value of about two billion dollars can not be ignored.[17]

The 1994 report found that the school system was not overcrowded but did not have excess space and suggested "new construction to replace obsolete buildings."[18] Of course, what is considered obsolete today might be cutting edge tomorrow, and caution might be advised since even the state Department of Education and the federal government change their standards routinely.

There is as yet no consensus on what kind of school building best supports the evolving approaches to education.[19]

With the usual Boston caution, the high schools that needed upgrading were examined. It was decided that these once state-of-the-art buildings were still serviceable and probably of more durable materials than those affordable in 1998. The suggested new construction was for additions to East Boston, Hyde Park, and Boston Latin High Schools while the interiors of these historic buildings were totally updated for current teaching programs. Consequently, those same high schools that had prepared their students for the economic complexities of the 1920s would once again be fully able to prepare their students for the twenty-first century.

Coming to terms with schools built in the 1970s was a major issue for Boston and for cities, suburbs, and towns across America. In many school systems, a major portion of the space was constructed in the 1960s and 1970s and, therefore, was decidedly modern in design.

After almost 20 years of operation, these [1970] buildings produce both strong positive examples and strong negative ones.[20]

The open plan classrooms were considered unworkable by 1994, and it was suggested that most be enclosed. The circulation patterns of the corridors were declared too complex with too many entry doors and hidden spaces. The new materials of grey concrete and metal panels were no longer prized above traditional red brick and limestone. On a larger scale, the campus plan high school envisioned and built in the 1970s was now considered too big and complex. In just one generation, people seemed to have forgotten and no longer understood the schools of the 1970s. The radical cutting edge report of 1962 that laid the groundwork for the 1970s had, in fact, created obsolescence in the minds of 1994 educators and architects. However, this is slowly changing as preservationists and architects begin to renovate, renew, and reinterpret these buildings; to understand the spirit of freedom, the thirst for new ideas, and the hope for the future that generated these designs. Though maybe too big, too open, too complex, and too different, these buildings might be appreciated again in the 2000s just as historic traditional schools were rediscovered in the late 1900s.

Another issue of the 1994 school evaluation report was termed "the small building dilemma," particularly for elementary schools.[21] It was noted that 50 of the 77 elementary schools "are either too small or marginally sufficient, to provide [state] recommended spaces for 250 to 350."[22] However, what is magical about 250 to 350 (or more) small children in one building is yet to be explained beyond monetary convenience by administrators or architects. In fact, as efforts intensify to increase test scores and comprehension for poor learners, class size is getting smaller and large schools are being divided into smaller house groups. In some instances, the small might be an advantage rather than a dilemma. William Brubaker in his book, *Planning and Designing Schools*, discussed this issue on a national level.

> *One of the most obvious problems with small schools is the presence of a very small faculty in each school. There is a possible answer, however, to the question of how to bring other resources into a small school to supplement the small staff and limited facilities: learning technology. Computers, television, distance learning, fax, laptops, telephones, and weekly visits to other education centers can make a small school as good as a larger school.*[23]

This proposed use of learning technology to augment facilities at smaller schools might be useful at some of Boston's small schools. Though technology can not substitute for indoor play areas to stretch arms and legs, it can help to broaden the learning experience for children of the future.

To ignore public schools is folly. In Boston, about 75% of the children attend public schools, and in many cities and suburbs, the percentage is yet greater.

> *More than 11 million of the 46 million children enrolled in America's public schools—about 24 percent—attend school in an urban district.*[24]

Boston is one of those many urban areas that is educating children in both new and old buildings. With thoughtfulness and purpose, this city created its schools throughout the century. With planning, talent, ingenuity, and some luck, it has produced school buildings that have been used and enjoyed by generations of diverse people. As the city continues its building program, new treasures are being created and existing treasures are being preserved. New early learning centers and rejuvenated high schools have been completed for the twenty-first century. New schools are being constructed and planned. With respect for the past, Boston is planning for a vibrant future. It is an unfinished story to be continued by future generations.

FOOTNOTES

1. Bradbury, Catherine, Case, Karl, Mayer, Christopher, "Chasing Good Schools in Massachusetts," *Regional Review,* Federal Reserve Bank of Boston, Q3, 198, Vol. 8, No. 3, p. 25.

2. Ibid, p. 26.

3. Wasserman, Miriam, "Snapshot of the Future: The Children of Immigrant America," *Regional Review,* Federal Reserve Bank of Boston, Q3, 1998, Vol. 8, No. 3, p. 23.

4. Agron, Joe, "The Urban Challenge: Meeting unique and diverse facility demands," AS&U, *American School & University,* July 1998, p. 18.

5. Hart, Jordan, Globe Staff, "School Chief Aims to End Racial Gap," *The Boston Globe,* October 29, 1998.

6. Wallace, Floyd, Associates, Inc., *Boston Public School Facilities Overview,* January 14, 1994, Phase 1: Volume 2 Inventory and Condition Report, p. 3.

7. Wasserman, op. cit., p. 21.

8. Ibid, p. 21.

9. Powers, John, "12 Moments that Mattered," *The Boston Globe Magazine,* March 2, 1997, p. 58.

10. Wasserman, op. cit., p. 22.

11. Ibid, p. 24.

12. Wallace, Floyd, Associates Inc., op. cit., p. 5.

13. Agron, op. cit., p. 19.

14. Wallace, Floyd, Associates Inc., op. cit., p. 3.

15. Wallace, Floyd, Associates Inc., *Boston Public Schools Facilities Overview,* Inventory and Condition Analysis, 1993, Volume I: Executive Summary, p. 2.

16. Radin, Charles A., "Bring Back the Burke," *The Boston Globe Magazine,* March 8, 1998, p. 24.

17. Wallace, Floyd, Volume I, op. cit., p. 4.

18. Ibid, p. 8.

19. Wallace Floyd Associates Inc., op. cit., p. 57.

20. Wallace Floyd Associates Inc., op. cit., p. 57.

21. Ibid, p. 51.

22. Wallace, Floyd, Volume I, op. cit., p. 8.

23. Brubaker, William G., *Planning and Designing Schools* (New York, McGraw-Hill, 1998) p. 40.

24. Agron, op. cit., p. 19.

6'-4"

Medallion Detail
East Boston High School
East Boston, 1926. Renovation and Addition 2001.

The 2001 renovation and addition by Cole and Goyette, Architects and Planners included a new gymnasium. The new brick facade was decorated with carved granite medallions representing the traditional and contemporary emblems of this school overlooking Boston Harbor.

Drawing courtesy of Cole and Goyette, Architects and Planners Inc.

List of Illustrations with Captions on CD-Rom

This is a list of illustrations with captions that are included on the CD-Rom which accompanies this book.

Map and Chart

1. Map of the City of Boston, Annual Report of the Department of School Buildings, January 1, 1935 to December 31, 1935.
   Illustration courtesy of Boston Public Schools.

2. Legislative History of Boston School Buildings, Annual Report of the Department of School Buildings, January 1, 1937 to December 31, 1937.
   Illustration courtesy of Boston Public Schools.

Margaret Fuller Elementary School, Jamaica Plain, 1892

3. Front Facade, Margaret Fuller Elementary School, Jamaica Plain, 1892.
   Photograph by Nick Wheeler.

4. Floor Plans, Margaret Fuller Elementary School, Jamaica Plain, 1892.
   Drawings courtesy of Cole and Goyette, Architects and Planners Inc.

William Howard Taft Middle School, Brighton, 1895

5. Exterior, William Howard Taft Middle School, Brighton, 1895.
   Photograph by Nick Wheeler.

Roger Clap Elementary School, Dorchester, 1896

6. Street Facade, Roger Clap Elementary School, Dorchester, 1896.
   Photograph by Nick Wheeler.

7. Fence Detail, Roger Clap Elementary School, Dorchester, 1896.
   Photograph by Nick Wheeler.

F. Lyman Winship Elementary School, Brighton, 1901

8. Drawing of Exterior, F. Lyman Winship Elementary School, Brighton, 1901. Annual Report of the Schoolhouse Department, February 1, 1923 to February 1, 1924. *Illustration courtesy of Boston Public Schools.*

9. Floor Plan, F. Lyman Winship Elementary School, Brighton, 1901. Annual Report of the Schoolhouse Department, February 1, 1923 to February 1, 1924. *Illustration courtesy of Boston Public Schools.*

10. Photograph of Addition, F. Lyman Winship Elementary School, Brighton, 1901. Annual Report of the Schoolhouse Department, February 1, 1924 to February 1, 1925. *Illustration courtesy of Boston Public Schools.*

11. Entry Facade, F. Lyman Winship Elementary School, Brighton, 1901.
    Photograph by Nick Wheeler.

William E. Russell Elementary School, Dorchester, 1903

12. Drawing of Exterior and Floor Plan, William E. Russell Elementary School, Dorchester, 1903. Annual Report of the Schoolhouse Department, February 1, 1902 to February 1, 1903.
   Illustration courtesy of Boston Public Schools.

13. Landscape Improvements, William E. Russell Elementary School, Dorchester, 1903. *Illustration courtesy of Boston Public Schools.*

14. Front Facade, William E. Russell Elementary School, Dorchester, 1903.
   Photograph by Nick Wheeler.

15. Entry Detail, William E. Russell Elementary School, Dorchester, 1903.
   Photograph by Nick Wheeler.

16. Classroom Seating, William E. Russell Elementary School, Dorchester, 1903. Annual Report of the Schoolhouse Department, February 1, 1924 to February 1, 1925. *Illustration courtesy of Boston Public Schools.*

Richard Mather Elementary School, Dorchester, 1905

17. Drawing of Exterior and Floor Plan, Richard Mather Elementary School, Dorchester, 1905. Annual Report of the Schoolhouse Department, January 31, 1903 to February 1, 1904. *Illustration courtesy of Boston Public Schools.*

18. Front Exterior, Richard Mather Elementary School, Dorchester, 1905.
   Photograph by Nick Wheeler.

19. Entry Court, Richard Mather Elementary School, Dorchester, 1905.
   Photograph by Nick Wheeler.

20. Exterior Details, Richard Mather Elementary School, Dorchester, 1905.
   Photograph by Nick Wheeler.

21. Parapet Detail, Richard Mather Elementary School, Dorchester, 1905.
   Photograph by Nick Wheeler.

Thomas Gardner Elementary School, Allston, 1906

22. Drawing of Exterior and Floor Plan, Thomas Gardner Elementary School, Allston, 1906. Annual Report of the Schoolhouse Department, January 31, 1903 to February 1, 1904. *Illustration courtesy of Boston Public Schools.*

23. Front Facade, Thomas Gardner Elementary School, Allston, 1906.
   Photograph by Richard Mandelkorn.

24. Play Yard Facade, Thomas Gardner Elementary School, Allston, 1906.
   Photograph by Richard Mandelkorn.

25. Assembly Hall, Thomas Gardner Elementary School, Allston, 1906.
   Photograph by Richard Mandelkorn.

26. Classroom, Thomas Gardner Elementary School, Allston, 1906.
   Photograph by Richard Mandelkorn.

27. Corridor, Thomas Gardner Elementary School, Allston, 1906.
   Photograph by Richard Mandelkorn.

William E. Endicott Elementary School, Dorchester, 1906

28. Drawing of Exterior and Floor Plan, William E. Endicott Elementary School, Dorchester, 1906. Annual Report of the Schoolhouse Department, February 1, 1904 to February 1, 1905.
Illustration courtesy of Boston Public Schools.

29. Front Facade, William E. Endicott Elementary School, Dorchester, 1906.
Photograph by Nick Wheeler.

30. Front Entry, William E. Endicott Elementary School, Dorchester, 1906.
Photograph by Nick Wheeler.

31. Lintel Detail, William E. Endicott Elementary School, Dorchester, 1906.
Photograph by Nick Wheeler.

32. Medallion, William E. Endicott Elementary School, Dorchester, 1906.
Photograph by Nick Wheeler.

Edward Everett Elementary School, Dorchester, 1909

33. Drawing of Exterior, Edward Everett Elementary School, Dorchester, 1909. Annual Report of the Schoolhouse Department, February 1, 1907 to February 1, 1908. *Illustration courtesy of Boston Public Schools.*

34. Front Facade, Edward Everett Elementary School, Dorchester, 1909.
Photograph by Richard Mandelkorn.

35. Assembly Hall, Edward Everett Elementary School, Dorchester, 1909.
Photograph by Richard Mandelkorn.

36. Classroom, Edward Everett Elementary School, Dorchester, 1909.
Photograph by Richard Mandelkorn.

Schoolhouse Standards, 1903–1906

37. Standards of General Detail, Annual Report of the Schoolhouse Department, January 31, 1903 to February 1, 1904.
Illustration courtesy of Boston Public Schools.

38. High School Standard Fittings, Annual Report of the Schoolhouse Department, February 1, 1905 to February 1, 1906.
Illustration courtesy of Boston Public Schools.

39. Sheet of Drawings, Annual Report of the Schoolhouse Department, February 1, 1905 to February 1, 1906. *Illustration courtesy of Boston Public Schools.*

Boston High School, Boston, 1911

40. Exterior, Boston High School, Boston, 1911. *Photographs by Doris Cole.*

Henry Dearborn Middle School, Roxbury, 1913

41. Drawing of Exterior, Henry Dearborn Middle School, Roxbury, 1913. Annual Report of the Schoolhouse Department, February 1, 1913 to February 1, 1914. *Illustration courtesy of Boston Public Schools.*

42. Entry Facade, Henry Dearborn Middle School, Roxbury, 1913. *Photographs by Doris Cole.*

John D. Philbrick Elementary School, Roslindale, 1913

43. Photograph of Exterior, John D. Philbrick Elementary School, Roslindale, 1913. Annual Report of the Schoolhouse Department, February 1, 1913 to February 1, 1914. *Photograph courtesy of Boston Public Schools.*

44. Entry Facade, John D. Philbrick Elementary School, Roslindale, 1913. *Photographs by Doris Cole.*

Emily A. Fifield Elementary School, Dorchester, 1918

45. Front Facade, Emily A. Fifield Elementary School, Dorchester, 1918. *Photographs by Doris Cole.*

Sarah Greenwood Elementary School, Dorchester, 1919

46. Front Facade, Sarah Greenwood Elementary School, Dorchester, 1919. *Photographs by Doris Cole.*

47. Drawing of Window Details, Sarah Greenwood Elementary School, Dorchester, 1919. *Drawing courtesy of Boston Public Schools, Campbell Center.*

Schoolhouse Standards, 1910–1915

48. High School Standard Fittings, Annual Report of the Schoolhouse Department, February 1, 1910 to February 1, 1911. *Illustration courtesy of Boston Public Schools.*

49. Standards of General Detail, Annual Report of the Schoolhouse Department, February 1, 1914 to February 1, 1915. *Illustration courtesy of Boston Public Schools.*

Boston Latin School, Boston, 1922

50. Exterior, Boston Latin School, Boston, 1922. Annual Report of the Schoolhouse Department, February 1, 1922 to February 1, 1923. *Photograph courtesy of Boston Public Schools*

Henry L. Higginson Elementary School, Roxbury, 1922

51. Playground Facade, Henry L. Higginson Elementary School, Roxbury, 1922. *Photograph by Richard Mandelkorn.*

52. Ground Floor, Henry L. Higginson Elementary School, Roxbury, 1922. *Photograph by Richard Mandelkorn.*

Rafael Hernandez Elementary School, Roxbury, 1923

53. Photograph of Exterior, Rafael Hernandez Elementary School, Roxbury, 1923. Annual Report of the Schoolhouse Department February 1, 1923 to February 1, 1924. *Photograph courtesy of Boston Public Schools.*

54. Entry Facade, Rafael Hernandez Elementary School, Roxbury, 1923. *Photograph by William T. Smith.*

55. Auditorium, Rafael Hernandez Elementary School, Roxbury, 1923. *Photograph by William T. Smith.*

Harriet A. Baldwin Elementary School, Brighton, 1926

56. Drawing of Exterior, Harriet A. Baldwin Elementary School, Brighton, 1926. Annual Report of the Schoolhouse Department February 1, 1925 to December 31, 1925. *Illustration courtesy of Boston Public Schools.*

57. Photograph of Exterior, Harriet A. Baldwin Elementary School, Brighton, 1926. Annual Report of the Schoolhouse Department, January 1, 1926 to December 31, 1926. *Photograph courtesy of Boston Public Schools.*

58. Exterior, Harriet A. Baldwin Elementary School, Brighton, 1926. *Photographs by Doris Cole.*

Thomas J. Kenny Elementary School, Dorchester, 1926

59. Drawing of Exterior, Thomas J. Kenny Elementary School, Dorchester, 1926. Annual Report of the Schoolhouse Department, February 1, 1925 to December 31, 1925. *Illustration courtesy of Boston Public Schools.*

60. Floor Plans, Thomas J. Kenny Elementary School, Dorchester, 1926. Annual Report of the Schoolhouse Department, February 1, 1925 to December 31, 1925. *Illustration courtesy of Boston Public Schools.*

William E. Channing Elementary School, Hyde Park, 1928

61. Exterior, William E. Channing Elementary School, Hyde Park, 1928. *Photographs by Doris Cole.*

Schoolhouse Standards, 1929

62. High School Standard Fittings, Annual Report of the Schoolhouse Department, January 1, 1929 to December 31, 1929. *Illustrations courtesy of Boston Public Schools.*

Brighton High School, Brighton, 1930

63. Drawing of Exterior, Brighton High School, 1930. Annual Report of the Schoolhouse Department, January 1, 1929 to December 31, 1929. *Illustrations courtesy of Boston Public Schools.*

64. Mural (completed 1934), Brighton High School, Brighton, 1930. *Photographs by Doris Cole.*

George H. Conley Elementary School, Roslindale, 1931

65. Exterior, George H. Conley Elementary School, Roslindale, 1931.
   Photographs by Doris Cole.

James J. Chittick Elementary School, Mattapan, 1931

66. Front Facade, James J. Chittick Elementary School, Mattapan, 1931.
   Photograph by Nick Wheeler.

Thomas A. Edison Middle School, Brighton, 1932

67. Main Entry, Exterior, Thomas A. Edison Middle School, Brighton, 1932.
   Photograph by Nick Wheeler.

68. Entry Doors, Thomas A. Edison Middle School, Brighton, 1932.
   Photograph by Nick Wheeler.

69. Door Detail, Thomas A. Edison Middle School, Brighton, 1932.
   Photograph by Nick Wheeler.

70. Light Standard at Main Entry, Thomas A. Edison Middle School,
   Brighton, 1932. *Photograph by Nick Wheeler.*

Jeremiah E. Burke High School, Dorchester, 1934

71. Auditorium Overview, Jeremiah E. Burke High School, Dorchester, 1934.
   Photograph by Nick Wheeler.

72. Auditorium Detail, Jeremiah E. Burke High School, Dorchester, 1934.
   Photograph by Nick Wheeler.

73. Decorative Grille Detail, Jeremiah E. Burke High School, Dorchester,
   1934. *Photograph by Nick Wheeler.*

74. Wood Paneling and Table, Jeremiah E. Burke High School, Dorchester,
   1934. *Photograph by Nick Wheeler.*

75. Commemorative Panel (completed 1946), Jeremiah E. Burke High
   School, Dorchester, 1934. *Photograph by Nick Wheeler.*

Patrick F. Gavin Middle School, South Boston, 1936

76. Drawing of Exterior, Patrick F. Gavin Middle School, South Boston, 1936.
   Annual Report of the Department of School Buildings, January 1, 1935
   to December 31, 1935. *Illustration courtesy of Boston Public Schools.*

77. Stair Hall Detail, Patrick F. Gavin Middle School, South Boston, 1936.
   Photograph by Nick Wheeler.

Washington Irving Middle School, Roslindale, 1936

78. Front Facade, Washington Irving Middle School, Roslindale, 1936.
   Photographs by Doris Cole.

79. Auditorium, Washington Irving Middle School, Roslindale, 1936.
   Photographs by Doris Cole.

Martin Luther King Jr. Middle School, Dorchester, 1937

80. Drawing, Martin Luther King Jr. Middle School, Dorchester, 1937.
Drawing courtesy of Boston Public Schools, Campbell Center.
81. Auditorium Detail, Martin Luther King Jr. Middle School, Dorchester, 1937. *Photograph by Nick Wheeler.*
82. Auditorium Seating, Martin Luther King Jr. Middle School, Dorchester, 1937. *Photograph by Nick Wheeler.*
83. Lobby Detail, Martin Luther King Jr. Middle School, Dorchester, 1937. *Photograph by Nick Wheeler.*

James P. Timilty Middle School, Roxbury, 1937

84. Front Entry, James P. Timilty Middle School, Roxbury, 1937. *Photograph by Nick Wheeler.*
85. Fire Escape Detail, James P. Timilty Middle School, Roxbury, 1937. *Photographs by Doris Cole.*
86. Auditorium, James P. Timilty Middle School, Roxbury, 1937. *Photographs by Doris Cole.*

Lucy Stone Elementary School, Dorchester, 1937

87. Drawing of Exterior, Lucy Stone Elementary School, Dorchester, 1937. Annual Report of the Department of School Buildings, January 1, 1935 to December 31, 1935. *Illustration courtesy of Boston Public Schools.*
88. Ground Floor Interior, Lucy Stone Elementary School, Dorchester, 1937. *Photograph by Richard Mandelkorn.*

Franklin D. Roosevelt Elementary School, Hyde Park, 1957

89. Front Facade, Franklin D. Roosevelt Elementary School, Hyde Park, 1957. *Photographs by Doris Cole.*

Patrick O'Hearn Elementary School, Dorchester, 1957

90. Floor Plan, Patrick O'Hearn Elementary School, Dorchester, 1957. *Drawing courtesy of Cole and Goyette, Architects and Planners Inc.*
91. Play Courtyard, Patrick O'Hearn Elementary School, Dorchester, 1957. *Photograph by Nick Wheeler.*
92. Classroom, Patrick O'Hearn Elementary School, Dorchester, 1957. *Photograph by Nick Wheeler.*
93. Auditorium, Patrick O'Hearn Elementary School, Dorchester, 1957. *Photograph by Nick Wheeler.*

Snowden International High School (conversion of the 1882 Boston Art Club), Boston, 1970

94. Exterior Facade, Snowden International High School (conversion of the 1882 Boston Art Club), Boston, 1970. *Photographs by Doris Cole.*

List of Boston Public Schools

The schools that are included on this list are those buildings that were designed as public schools and continued to be used as schools in the year 2001 (There is one exception on the list: The Snowden School, which was originally designed for the Boston Art Club). This is not intended to be a list of every public school or school program in Boston. The architect noted for each school was the architect for the original building only. However, most of these schools have received major renovations and additions over the years. Therefore, many architects have contributed their skills towards the design of each building.

1890–1899: 4 Schools
1892 Fuller Elementary School, 25 Glen Road, Jamaica Plain
    Architect: E.M. Wheelwright
1895 Taft Middle School, 20 Warren Street, Brighton
    Architect: E.M. Wheelwright
1896 Clap Elementary School, 35 Harvest Street, Dorchester
    Architect: William H. Besarick
1882 Snowden International School, 150 Newbury Street, Boston
    (originally designed for the Boston Art Club)
    Architect: William Ralph Emerson

1900–1909: 17 Schools
1900 Mary Lyon Elementary School, 50 Beechcroft Street, Brighton
    Architect: Richardson, Barott & Ferguson
1901 South Boston High School, 95 G Street, South Boston
    Architect: Herbert D. Hale
1901 Winship Elementary School, 54 Dighton Street, Brighton
    Architect: Whitman & Hood
1902 Rogers Middle School, 15 Everett Street, Hyde Park
    Architect: Loring & Phipps
1903 Russell Elementary School, 750 Columbia Road, Dorchester
    Architect: James Mulcahy
1904 Farragut Elementary School, 10 Fenwood Road, Boston
    Architect: Wheelwright & Haven
1904 Mendell Elementary School, 164 School Street, Roxbury
    Architect: Andrews, Jaques & Rantoul
1904 Perry Elementary School, 745 E. Seventh Street, South Boston
    Architect: Clough & Wardner

1904 Young Achievers Science & Math, 25 Walk Hill Street, Jamaica Plain
(originally the Francis Parkman Elementary School)
Architect: Perkins & Betton Architects
1905 Holmes Elementary School, 40 School Street, Dorchester
Architect: A.W. Longfellow
1905 Mason Elementary School, 150 Norfolk Avenue, Roxbury
Architect: John A. Fox
1905 Mather Elementary School, Meeting House Hill, Dorchester
Architect: Cram, Goodhue & Ferguson
1905 Otis Elementary School, 218 Marion Street, East Boston
Architect: Winslow & Bigelow
1906 Endicott Elementary School, 2 McLellan Street, Dorchester
Architect: James E. McLaughlin
1906 Gardner Elementary School, 30 Athol Street, Allston
Architect: Stickney & Austin
1909 Everett Elementary School, 71 Pleasant Street, Dorchester
Architect: E.T.P. Graham
1909 Hale Elementary School, 51 Cedar Street, Roxbury
Architect: Parker, Thomas & Rice

1910–1919: 11 Schools
1910 Adams Elementary School, 165 Webster Street, East Boston
Architect: Brigham, Coveney & Bisbee
1911 Boston High School, 152 Arlington Street, Boston
(originally the Abraham Lincoln Elementary School)
Architect: A.W. Longfellow
1911 Winthrop Elementary School, 35 Brookford Street, Dorchester
Architect: Maginnis & Walsh
1912 Lewis Middle School, 131 Walnut Avenue, Roxbury
Architect: Harrison H. Atwood
1913 Dearborn Middle School, 35 Greenville Street, Roxbury
(originally the High School of Practical Arts)
Architect: J.A. Schweinfurth
1913 Philbrick Elementary School, 40 Philbrick Street, Roslindale
Architect: Charles J. Bateman
1915 Dickerman Elementary School, 206 Magnolia Street, Roxbury
Architect: J.A. Schweinfurth
1918 Fifield Elementary School, 25 Dunbar Avenue, Dorchester
Architect: Harrison H. Atwood

1919 Sarah Greenwood Elementary & Middle School,
189 Glenway Street, Dorchester
Architect: Funk & Wilcox

1919 P.A. Shaw Elementary School, 429 Norfolk Street, Dorchester
Architect: James E. McLaughlin

1919 R. Shaw Middle School, 20 Mt. Vernon Street, West Roxbury
Architect: Blackwell, Clapp & Whittemore

1920–1929: 24 Schools

1921 Guild Elementary School, 195 Leyden Street, East Boston
Architect: Harrison H. Atwood

1922 Boston Latin School, 78 Avenue Louis Pasteur, Boston
Architect: James E. McLaughlin Architects

1922 Higginson Elementary School, 160 Harrishof Street, Roxbury
Architect: James H. Ritchie

1922 Thompson Middle School, 100 Maxwell Street, Dorchester
Architect: Harrison H. Atwood

1923 Hernandez Elementary & Middle School, 61 School Street, Roxbury
(originally the Theodore Roosevelt Intermediate School)
Architect: Joseph J. Driscoll

1923 McKinley Middle School, 50 St. Mary Street, Boston
Architect: Parker, Thomas & Rice

1924 Alighieri Elementary School, 37 Grove Street, Roxbury
Architect: James Purdon

1924 Emerson Elementary School, 6 Shirley Street, Roxbury
Architect: Mulhall & Holmes

1924 Hamilton Elementary School, 198 Strathmore Road, Brighton
Architect: Coolidge & Shattuck

1925 Beethoven Elementary School, 5125 Washington Street, West Roxbury
Architect: William W. Drummey

1925 Cleveland Middle School, 11 Charles Street, Dorchester
Architect: O'Connell & Shaw

1925 Dorchester High School, 9 Peacevale Road, Dorchester
Architect: Harris Atwood

1925 Garfield Elementary School, 95 Beechcroft Street, Brighton
Architect: John F. Cullen

1926 Baldwin Elementary School, 121 Corey Road, Brighton
Architect: Fay, Spofford & Thorndike

1926 Boston Latin Academy, 205 Townsend Street, Boston
(originally the Roxbury Memorial High School)
Architect: Harris Atwood

1926 East Boston High School, 86 White Street, East Boston
  Architect: John M. Gray Company
1926 Kenny Elementary School, 19 Oakton Avenue, Dorchester
  Architect: John M. Gray Company
1926 McKay Elementary & Middle School, 122 Cottage Street, East Boston
  Architect: Charles R. Greco
1926 Perkins Elementary School, 50 Burke Street, South Boston
  Architect: Frank I. Cooper Corporation
1928 Channing Elementary School, 35 Sunnyside Street, Hyde Park
  Architect: John M. Gray Company
1929 Bates Elementary School, 426 Beech Street, Roslindale
  Architect: Newell & Blevins
1929 Hyde Park High School, 655 Metropolitan Avenue, Hyde Park
  Architect: McLaughlin & Burr Architects
1929 Wheatley Middle School, 20 Kearsage Avenue, Roxbury
  (originally the Horace Mann School for the Deaf)
  Architect: John M. Gray Company
1929 McKinley Vocational High School, 97 Peterborough Street, Boston
  (originally the Martin Milmore Elementary School)
  Architect: George Ernest Robinson, Architect

1930–1939: 22 Schools

1930 Brighton High School, 25 Warren Street, Brighton
  Architect: O'Connell & Shaw
1930 Lewenberg Middle School, 20 Outlook Road, Mattapan
  Architect: Desmond & Lord
1931 Chittick Elementary School, 154 Ruskindale Road, Mattapan
  Architect: M.A. Dyer Company
1931 Conley Elementary School, 450 Poplar Street, Roslindale
  Architect: William W. Drumney
1931 Mary Curley Middle School, 493 Centre Street, Jamaica Plain
  Architect: McLaughlin & Burr
1931 Sumner Elementary School, 15 Basile Street, Roslindale
  Architect: Dana Somes Architect
1931 Taylor Elementary School, 1060 Morton Street, Mattapan
  Architect: Department of School Buildings
1932 Edison Middle School, 60 Glenmont Road, Brighton
  Architect: Allbright & Blaney
1932 Edwards Middle School, 28 Walker Street, Charlestown
  Architect: John M. Gray Company

1932 Eliot Elementary School, 16 Charter Street, Boston
    Architect: Charles R. Greco
1932 Ellis Elementary School, 302 Walnut Avenue, Roxbury
    Architect: Fay, Spofford & Thorndike
1932 Mozart Elementary School, 236 Beech Street, Roslindale
    Architect: Harold R. Duffie
1932 O'Donnell Elementary School, 33 Trenton Street, East Boston
    Architect: Department of School Buildings
1932 Wilson Middle School, 18 Croftland Avenue, Dorchester
    Architect: John M. Gray Company
1933 Patrick Kennedy Elementary School, 343 Saratoga Street, East Boston
    Architect: Desmond & Lord
1934 Burke High School, 60 Washington Street, Dorchester
    (originally the Jeremiah E. Burke High School for Girls)
    Architect: George Ernest Robinson
1935 Kilmer Elementary School, 35 Baker Street, West Roxbury
    Architect: Harrison H. Atwood
1936 Gavin Middle School, 215 Dorchester Street, South Boston
    Architect: John M. Gray Company
1936 Irving Middle School, 105 Cummins Highway, Roslindale
    Architect: Sturgis Associates
1937 King Middle School, 77 Lawrence Avenue, Dorchester
    (originally the Patrick T. Campbell Junior High School)
    Architect: Funk & Wilcox
1937 Stone Elementary School, 22 Regina Road, Dorchester
    Architect: Frank I. Cooper, Corp.
1937 Timilty Middle School, 205 Roxbury Street, Roxbury
    Architect: M.A. Dyer Company

1940–1949: 1 School
1941 Manning Elementary School, 130 Louders Lane, Jamaica Plain
    Architect: William Stanley Parker & Sturgis Associates, Inc.

1950–1959: 8 Schools
1957 Dever Elementary School, 325 Mt. Vernon Street, Dorchester
    Architect: Thomas F. McDonough
1957 Elihu Greenwood Elementary School,
    612 Metropolitan Avenue, Hyde Park
    Architect: John M. Gray Company
1957 O'Hearn Elementary School, 1669 Dorchester Avenue, Dorchester
    Architect: Richmond & Goldberg

1957 Franklin Roosevelt Elementary School, 95 Needham Road, Hyde Park
    Architect: Campbell & Aldrich
1957 McKinley Schools, 90 Warren Avenue, Boston
    (originally the Charles E. Mackey School)
    Architect: Thomas F. McDonough
1958 Bradley Elementary School, 110 Beachview Road, East Boston
    Architect: Desmond & Lord
1958 Grew Elementary School, 40 Gordon Avenue, Hyde Park
    Architect: John Guarino, AIA, Architect
1959 Tobin Elementary & Middle School, 40 Smith Street, Roxbury
    Architect: Coletti Brothers

1960–1969: 5 Schools

1961 Hurley Elementary School, 70 Worcester Street, Boston
    Architect: John M. Gray Company
1963 John Kennedy Elementary School, 7 Bolster Street, Jamaica Plain
    Architect: M.A. Dyer
1963 Warren-Prescott Elementary School, 50 School Street, Charlestown
    Architect: W. Chester Browne and Associates
1967 McCormack Middle School, 315 Mt. Vernon Street, Dorchester
    Architect: T. F. McDonough, FAIA and J. M. Gray Co. Architects of Record
1969 Trotter Elementary School, 135 Humboldt Avenue, Dorchester
    Architect: Drummey Rosane Anderson Inc.

1970–1979: 23 Schools

1970 J. Curley Elementary School, 40 Pershing Road, Jamaica Plain
    Architect: Haldeman & Goransson Associates Inc.
1971 Carter Center School, 396 Northampton Street, Roxbury
    Architect: Boston Public Facilities Department
1971 Haley Elementary School, 570 American Legion Highway, Roslindale
    Architect: Coletti Brothers Inc.
1971 Harvard-Kent Elementary School, 50 Bunker Hill Street, Charlestown
    Architect: Flansburgh Associates Inc.
1971 Lee Elementary School, 155 Talbot Avenue, Dorchester
    Architect: Isidor Richmond and Carney Goldberg
1971 Marshall Elementary School, 35 Westville Street, Dorchester
    Architect: Whitney Atwood Norcross Associates Inc.
1972 Agassiz Elementary School, 20 Child Street, Jamaica Plain
    Architect: Environmental Systems International Architects (E. Flansburgh)
1972 Hennigan Elementary School, 200 Heath Street, Jamaica Plain
    Architect: PARD Team

1972 Holland Elementary School, 85 Olney Street, Dorchester
　　Architect: Benjamin Thompson & Associates Inc.
1972 Ohrenberger Elementary School,
　　175 West Boundary Road, West Roxbury
　　Architect: Charles A. Maguire & Associates Inc.
1972 Tynan Elementary School, 650 E. Fourth Street, South Boston
　　(originally the Hart Dean Elementary School)
　　Architect: Chapman and Goyette Associates Inc.
1973 Murphy Elementary School, 1 Worrell Street, Dorchester
　　Architect: Samuel Glaser & Partners, Architects
1975 Blackstone Elementary School, 380 Shawmut Avenue, Boston
　　Architect: Stull Associates Inc.
1975 Condon Elementary School, 200 D Street, South Boston
　　Architect: Whitney Atwood Norcross Associates Inc.
1975 Jackson Mann Elementary School, 40 Armington Street, Allston
　　Architect: Pierce & Pierce, Korslund LeNormand & Quann Inc.
1975 Umana/Barnes Middle School, 312 Border Street, East Boston
　　Architect: Eisenberg & Schiffer Associates, Architects
1976 Quincy Elementary School, 885 Washington Street, Boston
　　Architect: The Architects Collaborative, Inc.
1976 West Roxbury High School, 1205 V.F.W. Parkway, West Roxbury
　　Architect: Samuel Glaser and Partners Inc.
1977 Mattahunt Elementary School, 100 Hebron Street, Mattapan
　　Architect: Parsons Brinckerhoff Quade & Douglas Inc.
1978 Charlestown High School, 240 Medford Street, Charlestown
　　Architect: Hill Miller Friedlaeder Hollander Inc.
1978 Madison Park High School, 55 New Dudley Street, Roxbury
　　Architect: Marcel Breuer and Tician Papachristou
1978 O'Bryant High School, 55 New Dudley Street, Roxbury
　　(originally the Boston Technical High School)
　　Architect: Marcel Breuer and Tician Papacristou
1979 English High School, 144 McBride Street, Jamaica Plain
　　(originally the Jamaica Plain High School)
　　Architect: Pierce, Pierce & Kramer, Korslund LeNormand & Quann Inc.

1981–2001: 3 Schools
1998 Early Education Center, 108 Babson Street, Mattapan
　　Architect: TAMS Consultants Inc.
1998 Early Education Center, 35 Gove Street, East Boston
　　Architect: HMFH Architects, Inc.
1998 Early Education Center, 263 Blue Hill Avenue, Roxbury
　　Architect: Leers Weinzapfel Associates Inc.

Bibliography

Allen, Frederick Lewis, *Only Yesterday: An Informal History of the Nineteen-Twenties* (New York, Harper 4 Brothers Publishers 1931).

Agron, Joe, "The Urban Challenge: Meeting Unique and Diverse Facility Demands," *AS&U, American School & University*, July 1998.

Boston Evening Transcript, "Brighton High Murals," September 15, 1934.

Boston Public Schools, *Introducing the Boston Public Schools: A Guide for Parents and Students*, 1996.

Boston Public Schools, *Introducing the Boston Public Schools: A Guide for Parents and Students*, 1997.

Boston Public Schools, *The Boston Public Schools at a Glance*, BPS Facts, No. 1, March 1999.

Boston Seniority, "WPA Art," January 1983.

Boston Schools—1962: A Report On The Schools of Boston, This study was undertaken under a contract between the Boston Redevelopment Authority and Harvard University and with the cooperation of the Mayor, the School Committee, and the School Buildings Commission of the City of Boston, May 1962.

Bradbury, Katherine, Case, Karl, and Mayer, Christopher, "Chasing Good Schools in Massachusetts," *Regional Review*, Federal Reserve Bank of Boston, Q3, 1998, Vol. 8, No. 3.

Brubaker, C. William, *Planning and Designing Schools* (New York, McGraw-Hill, 1998).

Carter, Paul A, *Another Part of the Twenties* (New York, Columbia University Press, 1977).

City of Boston, Office of the City Clerk, Archives & Records Management Division.
  * Annual Reports of the Department of School Buildings 1907–1965, Box #3C85
  * Boston School Department Photographs, 92042, Box 1 of 2, 6K 012
  * Boston School Department Photographs, 92042, Box 2 of 2, 6K 012
  * Boston School Department Photographs, 92042, Box 3 of 3, 6K 011

Cole, Doris, *From Tipi to Skyscraper, a History of Women in Architecture*, (Boston, i press, 1973).

Cole, Doris and Taylor, Karen Cord, *The Lady Architects: Lois Lilley Howe, Eleanor Manning and Mary Almy, 1893–1937*, (New York, Midmarch Arts Press, 1990).

Cole and Goyette, Architects and Planners Inc., *Community Learning Center/New K-8 School, Boston, Massachusetts, Building and Site Program*, prepared for City of Boston Public Facilities Department, November 16, 1995.

Community Learning Centers, Blue Ribbon Commission, School Buildings Capital Master Plan, Volume 1—Summary, Mayor Thomas M. Menino, August 1995.

Daley, Beth, Globe Staff, "Schools have gone downhill since busing? Don't believe it," *The Boston Sunday Globe*, Focus Section, February 21, 1999.

Daley, Beth, Globe Staff, "School's Offer Just Too Good to Refuse," *The Boston Globe*, Learning Section, September 27, 1998

Encyclopædia Britannica, (Chicago, Encyclopædia Britannica, Inc., William Benton, Publishers, 1962).

Faulkner, Harold Underwood, *A History of American Life: Volume XI, A Quest for Social Justice: 1898–1914* (New York, The MacMillan Company, 1931).

Fitch, James Marston, *Walter Gropius*, (New York, George Braziller, Inc, 1960).

Formisano, Ronald P., *Boston Against Busing* (Chapel Hill, The University of North Carolina Press, 1991).

Hart, Jordan, Globe Staff, "School Chief Aims to End Racial Gap," *Boston Globe*, October 29, 1998.

Kelley, Walt, *What They Never Told You About Boston (Or What They Did That Were Lies)*, (Camden, Maine, Down East Books, 1993).

Lucas, J. Anthony, *Common Ground*, (New York, Alfred A. Knopf, 1985)

Massachusetts Department of Education, *Regulations Governing The School Building Assistance Act, Chapter 645 of the Acts of 1948, As Amended*, Dr. Robert V. Antonucci, Commissioner of Education, July 1996.

Meltzer, Milton, *Violins & Shovels, The WPA Arts Project* (New York, Delacorte Press, 1976).

Mulvoy Jr., Thomas F., "Buses and Bitterness," *The Boston Globe Magazine*, March 1997.

O'Loughlin, John (Ed.), *What's In a Name? Names of Boston's Public Elementary and Middle Schools: Their Origins* (Boston, School Volunteers for Boston, Inc. and Boston Public Schools, May 1980).

Radin, Charles A., "Bringing Back the Burke," *The Boston Globe Magazine*, March 8, 1998.

Russell, Francis, *The Great Interlude* (New York, McGraw-Hill Book Company, 1964).

Schlereth, Thomas J., *Victorian America: Transformations in Everyday Life, 1876–1915* (New York, Harper Collins Publishers, 1991).

Slosson, Preston William, *The Great Crusade and After* 1914–1918 (New York, The MacMillan Company, 1930).

Southworth, Susan and Michael, *The Boston Society of Architects' AIA Guide to Boston* (Chester, Connecticut, The Globe Pequot Press, 1992).

Speer, Albert, *Inside the Third Reich*, (New York, Avon Books, 1971).

The School Committee of the City of Boston, *Directory of Boston Public Schools*, September 1995.

Time-Life Books Editors, *This Fabulous Century* 1900–1910, Volume I (New York, Time-Life Books, 1971).

"12 Moments That Mattered 1872–1997," *The Boston Globe Magazine*, March 2, 1997.

Torre, Susana (Ed.), *Women in American Architecture: A Historic and Contemporary Perspective*, (New York, Whitney Library of Design, 1977).

Trout, Charles H., Boston, *The Great Depression and the New Deal* (New York, Oxford University Press, 1977).

United States Division of Information, America Builds, *The Record of the PWA* (Washington, United States Printing Office, 1939).

Wallace, Floyd, Associates, Inc., *Boston Public School Facilities Overview, Inventory and Conditions Analysis, Volume I: Executive Summary, Volume 2: Inventory and Condition Report, Volume 3: Facility Profiles*, prepared for City of Boston Public Facilities Department and Boston Public School Department, 1993.

Wasserman, Miriam and Goodman, John, photographs, "Snapshot of the Future: The Children of Immigrant America," *Regional Review*, Federal Reserve Bank of Boston, Q3, 1998, Vol. 8, No. 3

Whitehill, Walter Muir, Boston: A *Topographical History* (Cambridge, The Belknap Press of Harvard University, 1968).

Index

Author's Biographies

DORIS COLE is a licensed architect and author of several books and numerous essays on historic architecture. Her previous books include *Eleanor Raymond, Architect*, *From Tipi to Skyscraper: A History of Women in Architecture* and *The Lady Architects: Howe, Manning and Almy 1893–1937*. She has contributed essays to *Pilgrims and Pioneers: New England Women in the Arts* and *Women in American Architecture: A Historic and Contemporary Perspective*. As president of Cole and Goyette, Architects and Planners Inc., Ms. Cole has designed the renovations/rejuvenations at more than a dozen Boston Public Schools. In 1992, she was included on the Massachusetts Honor Roll of Innovation and Discovery for her innovative renovations to Massachusetts Public Schools. In 1994, Ms. Cole was named a Fellow of the American Institute of Architects for her professional achievements. Doris Cole was educated in the public schools of Chicago, Illinois, and Grand Rapids, Michigan. She received the A.B. cum laude from Radcliffe College and the Master of Architecture from Harvard University Graduate School of Design.

NICK WHEELER is a nationally acclaimed architectural photographer. He has been commissioned to photograph notable buildings, including schools and historic buildings throughout the United States. Nick Wheeler's photographs have been published in numerous books and magazines throughout the world including *Time*, *Life*, *Architectural Digest*, and *Newsweek* magazines, the *Encyclopædia Britannica*, and many architectural monographs. His photographs have been exhibited at the Massachusetts Institute of Technology, Katonah Museum of Art, New York Museum of Modern Art, the American Institute of Architects in Washington, D.C., and the Boston Society of Architects. In 1985, Mr. Wheeler was awarded the American Institute of Architects Honor for Career Achievement. In 1992, he was honored with the exhibition "The Indelible Image: The Architectural Photographs of Nick Wheeler" at the American Institute of Architects and the Boston Society of Architects. Nick Wheeler was born in Boston and received the B.A. in Architecture from Stanford University.

The Boston Preservation Alliance

THE BOSTON PRESERVATION ALLIANCE was established in 1978. It began as the City Conservation League on a picket line to save the Jordan Marsh block in the spring of 1975. Three years later, this first grassroots historic preservation advocacy group in Boston grew into the Boston Preservation Alliance together with 25 other representatives of preservation organizations. An informal association at first, the Alliance strengthened in numerous advocacy battles throughout the years to become an incorporated nonprofit organization with a major say in the city's historic landscape.

The organization's first newsletter, the *AllianceLetter*, was published in April 1980 and has continued to be an effective tool to stir public awareness. The Alliance was granted nonprofit 501(c)(3) IRS status in the spring of 1982. In 1983, Rupert A. M. Davis became the first executive director of the Alliance and Susan Park became the chairman. The Alliance frequently changed addresses until 1984 when it moved to the historic Old City Hall at 45 School Street in Boston. In 2001, the executive director, Albert Rex, continues the Alliance advocacy and educational programs.

The advocacy issues addressed by the Boston Preservation Alliance have encompassed specific buildings and the effect upon neighboring areas. The Alliance's active involvement helped to save the historic buildings in the Theater District from demolition; was effective in saving the facade of the Boston Stock Exchange Building; and was instrumental in relocation rather than demolishing the Resident Physician's House at the Massachusetts General Hospital.

The educational activities of the Boston Preservation Alliance began in the late 1980s. Over the years, the Alliance has offered a variety of study tours to historic Rhode Island Farms, Portland, Maine, the Hudson River Valley, Charleston, South Carolina, and walking tours of Boston. In 1988, the Alliance established the first preservation award program in Boston. The award categories have varied over the years to reflect the challenges facing developers and city agencies. The winners have included the Berkley Building, the African Meeting House, East Boston High School, and many other notable historic buildings in Boston, Massachusetts.

Instructions for Use of the CD-Rom

The CD found in the back of the book contains 106 photographs, drawings, and charts for *School Treasures*. To access these images you need to have the program Adobe Acrobat Reader 3.0 or higher installed on your computer. This program is free from Adobe and for your convenience we have included the PC version of Acrobat Reader 5.0 on this CD. To install Acrobat Reader on your computer, follow the directions below.

System Requirements for Acrobat Reader 5.0 for Computers Running Under Windows*
- Intel Pentium processor
- Microsoft Windows 95 OSR 2.0, Windows 98 SE, Windows Millennium Edition, Windows NT 4.0 with Service Pack 5, Windows 2000, or Windows XP
- 64 MB RAM
- 24 MB of available hard-disk space

Installation Instructions
- Turn on your computer and insert the CD into your CD drive with the label face up. Close the CD-Rom drive.
- Be certain to close all programs that may be running before continuing.
- Double click on the icon "My Computer" and then double-click on your CD drive that should now be labeled "School Treasures."
- You will see three files listed on your screen: (1) Acrobat Reader.exe; (2) Instructions for Use of the CD-Rom.txt; and (3) School Treasures.pdf.
- Double click the Acrobat Reader.exe file and follow the installation and setup instructions provided on your computer screen.
- Upon completion of the installation of Acrobat Reader you will need to restart your computer.

---

*If your computer does not meet these requirements, you can download an alternate version of Adobe Acrobat Reader from the Adobe web site (www.adobe.com/products/acrobat/alternate.html).

Viewing Instructions

Once you have installed Acrobat Reader on your computer you can view the photographs, drawings and charts by double clicking on the file entitled School Treasures.pdf. This will automatically launch Acrobat Reader. The Bookmarks have been set up as links to each school. The number in parentheses ( ) next to each Bookmark refers to the number of images on this CD for each school. The Table of Contents has also been linked to each image on the CD and will enable you to locate a specific school photograph by double clicking on the title and description for that particular image.

Please be aware that the images on this CD cannot be copied or printed or used for any purpose other than viewing.

A FRIDAY NIGHT LIGHTS COMPANION

LOVE, LOSS, AND FOOTBALL IN DILLON, TEXAS

Edited by Leah Wilson

 AN IMPRINT OF BENBELLA BOOKS, INC. DALLAS, TEXAS

Smart Pop is an Imprint of BenBella Books, Inc.
10300 N. Central Expressway, Suite 400
Dallas, TX 75231
www.benbellabooks.com
www.smartpopbooks.com
Send feedback to feedback@benbellabooks.com

Printed in the United States of America
1098754321

Library of Congress Cataloging-in-Publication Data is available for this title.
ISBN 978-1- 935618-56-0

Copyediting by Erica Lovett
Proofreading by Michael Fedison
Cover design by Faceout Studio
Text design and composition by Neuwirth & Associates, Inc.
Printed by Bang Printing

Distributed by Perseus Distribution
http://www.perseusdistribution.com/

To place orders through Perseus Distribution:
Tel: (800) 343-4499
Fax: (800) 351-5073
E-mail: orderentry@perseusbooks.com

Significant discounts for bulk sales are available. Please contact Glenn Yeffeth at glenn@benbellabooks.com or (214) 750-3628.